The Shattered Peloton

The
Shattered
Peloton

The Devastating Impact of World War I
on the Tour de France

GRAHAM HEALY

BREAKAWAY BOOKS
HALCOTTSVILLE, NEWYORK
2014

The Shattered Peloton:
The Devastating Impact of World War I on the Tour de France
Copyright © 2014 by Graham Healy

ISBN: 978-1-62124-011-2
Library of Congress Control Number: 2014936934

Published by Breakaway Books
P. O. Box 24
Halcottsville, NY 12438
breakawaybooks.com

FIRST EDITION

Contents

Prologue 11

1. The 1914 Tour 21

2. A Call to Arms 39

3. The Rape of Belgium 49

4. A Clash with Desgrange 59

5. The Foreign Legionnaire 71

6. Survivor 87

7. The Aussies 93

8. The Fighter Pilot 103

9. A Sense of Normality 121

10. Death in the Skies 129

11. The Italian Front 143

12. The Elegant Argentinean 159

13. The Youngest Rider 177

14. *Lanterne Rouge* 187

15. Sentenced to Death 195

16. Armistice 203

17. A New Beginning 211

Bibliography 219

ACKNOWLEDGMENTS

I would like to thank Garth Battista at Breakaway Books for his faith in this book, and his help along the way. For their valuable feedback, I would like to thank my brother David, John Marron, and my wife Nina. For his help with the book cover design, thanks go to David Gill.

Prologue

In the early hours of Sunday, June 28, 1914, a large group of cyclists assembled in Saint-Cloud, a suburb of Paris about ten kilometers from the center of the city. The 145 riders were lining up to start the first stage of the twelfth edition of the Tour de France. Even though the race had been instituted just a decade previously, and had experienced some serious teething problems, it was ever-increasingly popular. The Tour had already become an integral part of the French sporting calendar. It was unpredictable and chaotic, and the inevitable drama, joy, and heartache in the race captured the imagination of the French public.

Despite the unsociable hour, there was still a sizable crowd of onlookers, eager to see the top cyclists of the day in the flesh. Like the previous year's race, the 1914 Tour was traveling in a counterclockwise direction; competitors would hit the Pyrénées before the Alps, covering 5,405 kilometers over fifteen stages. There were a number of favorites for the race, including the winner of the previous year's edition, the Belgian Philippe Thys. However, the partisan spectators were hopeful that one of their men, possibly Henri Pélissier who had won the previous year's Tour of Lombardy or Eugène Christophe who had come close to winning the previous year's race, could take the title instead.

145 riders would set off at the start
of the twelfth edition of the Tour de France.

It was a very strong lineup for the race that year, with seven previous winners taking part: the aforementioned Thys along with Frenchmen Louis Trousselier, Gustave Garrigou, Lucien Petit-Breton, and Octave Lapize; François Faber from Luxembourg; and the Belgian Odile Defraye. In addition four future Tour winners were taking part.

The race departed from Saint-Cloud at 3 AM with a peloton consisting of seventy-one professionals and seventy-four *isolés*—the class of cyclist without a sponsor. The Tour was starting off with a mammoth 388-kilometer stage to Le Havre. Little did the cyclists know as they rolled off from the start line, however, that an event that day on the opposite side of the Continent would change all of their lives forever.

Hostility had been building in Europe in the past number of years, with a number of different alliances forming among the major military powers. France had aligned with Russia initially in 1892 and later with Great Britain to form the Triple Entente, while Germany, Austria-Hungary, and Italy had formed the Triple Alliance.

Tensions between France and Germany had actually served as the backdrop to the creation of the Tour de France. In 1894 a young French soldier of Jewish descent by the name of Alfred Dreyfus was convicted of selling military secrets to the Germans—a scandal that would divide French opinion. The Dreyfus family had originated in Alsace, which had been annexed by Germany after the Franco-Prussian War. In the following years the family would move to Paris, and German would be their first language.

In 1894 French counter-intelligence realized that secrets were being passed to the Germans. The finger of suspicion was pointed at Alfred Dreyfus. It was said that he was the prime suspect because German was his first language, but also because of anti-Semitism within the French army. He was convicted in a court-martial and sentenced to life imprisonment on Devil's Island in French Guiana. Dreyfus would be proven innocent years later when new evidence emerged, which the military had tried to suppress. He later served in World War One with great distinction.

Debates emerged about Dreyfus's innocence, and members of the French public were divided in their opinion. Those on the anti-Dreyfus side would be accused by some of anti-Semitism. A division also emerged within the press, as many employees of France's most popular sports newspaper, *Le Vélo*, were anti-Dreyfussards; they broke away to form the rival newspaper *L'Auto-Vélo* in 1900. The owner of *Le Vélo* won a court case forcing *L'Auto-Vélo* to change its name, which it subsequently did, to *L'Auto*. This change in name saw sales plummet rapidly. It was against this backdrop that the Tour de France was conceived.

The first Tour de France was run in 1903 as the brainchild of Géo Lefèvre, the cycling correspondent of *L'Auto*. In November 1902 Lefèvre and the editor of the newspaper, Henri Desgrange, went for lunch at the Zimmer Madrid on Boulevard Montmartre. There Desgrange explained that they were looking for new ways to help increase sales, and Lefèvre suggested that *L'Auto* should hold a six-day race similar to those on tracks around Europe and North America. However, instead of being held in a velodrome, this race would be on the roads around France. Desgrange said, "As I understand it, petit Géo, you are suggesting a Tour de France."

Another rival newspaper, *Le Petit Journal*, had organized the epic twelve-hundred-kilometer bicycle race Paris–Brest–Paris in 1891; it had been an immediate success, with a considerable increase in sales. The first long-distance race from Paris to Rouen had been organized by cycling magazine *Le Vélocipède Illustré* as early as 1869. Through organizing and sponsoring a race, a particular newspaper would become the best source of information for cycling fans hoping to learn how the event was progressing, and would therefore see a boost in sales.

One of the major problems that *Le Petit Journal* had encountered with Paris–Brest–Paris was that the logistics of organizing the race had been so difficult that they decided it could only be held once every ten years. The Tour de France, on the other hand, was intended to be run as an annual event, so it would require considerably more support.

Two months after the idea was first suggested, the race was announced in the pages of *L'Auto*. The newspaper claimed it was going to be "the greatest cycling trial in the entire world. A race more than a month long: Paris to Lyon to Marseille to Toulouse to Bordeaux to Nantes to Paris." The French public was immediately intrigued.

Seventy-eight riders originally signed up to take part, but as the start date grew closer, quite a few dropped out—due to fear of the unknown, lack of training, or various other reasons. On the July 1,

1903, fifty French riders and ten foreigners lined up outside the Café au Reveil-Matin in Montgeron south of Paris to start the first Tour. Desgrange agreed to pay the expenses of all the riders who took part, hoping the increase in newspaper sales would easily cover this outlay. The longest stage of the race was the final stage from Nantes to Paris, which was an incredible 471 kilometers; the shortest, from Toulouse to Bordeaux, was still 268 kilometers.

Nearly three weeks later, on July 19, twenty-one riders arrived back at the Parc des Princes velodrome in Paris. An estimated twenty thousand spectators witnessed Maurice Garin win the final stage, and also the race overall. The first Tour had been an incredible success. Daily sales of *L'Auto* had increased from twenty thousand to thirty thousand in the buildup to the race, and had gone up to sixty-five thousand during the race itself.

Soon after the finish, Desgrange had already started planning the following year's race. This second edition would prove a lot more problematic, however, as cheating was rife. Cyclists were accused of having taken trains during stages, using the slipstream of cars, and sabotaging competitor's bicycles, among other underhanded methods.

The Tour nearly came to an end after that second edition, but Desgrange persevered, and the race went on from strength to strength. Its format was ever-evolving, with different changes every year. Some of them worked, some didn't. The only significant change for the 1914 race was that all of the competitors would have their race numbers fixed to their frames, which would make it easier for judges, journalists, and spectators alike to identify everybody.

On the same day as the opening stage of the 1914 Tour, Archduke Franz Ferdinand of the Austro-Hungarian Empire was visiting Sarajevo in Bosnia to inspect the armed forces stationed there. His country had annexed the small Balkan nation in 1908, much to the chagrin of neighboring Serbia. Traveling with the archduke was his wife, Sophie, Duchess of Hohenberg, who had been denied royal status, as she was not a member of one of the reigning or formerly reigning dynasties of Europe. Their union had caused much outrage within the imperial family. The archduke wasn't a particularly popular man, especially in the Balkans. He was said to have looked down on southern Slavs, apparently calling them "subhuman." One of the first mistakes made was that his trip to Bosnia was announced in March, giving anyone time to plot his assassination.

While the riders in the Tour were nearing Abbeville in the Somme department, nearly two hundred kilometers north of Paris, the archduke and duchess were traveling through the streets of Sarajevo in an open-top car when Serbian nationalist Nedeljko Cabrinovic threw a bomb at their car. It bounced off the back of the vehicle, and the explosion injured some bystanders and a soldier, but the royal couple were unharmed. It would later emerge that Cabrinovic was a member of the nationalist group Mlada Bosna (Young Bosnia), which was

Archduke Franz Ferdinand of Austria, with his wife Sophie,
Duchess of Hohenberg and their children. Both the Archduke
and Sophie would be killed by Gavrilo Princip.

supported by the Serbian militant group Black Hand. Their objective
was to break off from the Austro-Hungarian Empire and become
part of a Greater Serbia or Yugoslavia.

A visibly shaken archduke then attended a reception at the town hall, and afterward the group decided to visit the hospital where the wounded from the earlier bombing had been taken. The convoy set off again. Unfortunately the driver took a wrong turn into Franz Josef Street, where a nineteen-year-old named Gavrilo Princip stood. He was also a member of the Young Bosnia group. Princip fired two shots into the car at point-blank range, with one hitting the archduke in the jugular vein and the other hitting his wife in the abdomen. Princip then tried to kill himself but was wrestled to the ground before he could do so. Both the archduke and Sophie were dead within half an hour. Another member of the traveling party, Count Harrach, said that the archduke's last words were, "Sophie, Sophie! Don't die! Live for our children!"

As the couple lay dying, the Tour de France continued toward Le Havre. There hadn't been a considerable amount of action in the stage, but with fifty kilometers remaining, two previous winners, Octave Lapize and Lucien Petit-Breton, attempted to break away along with Émile Georget. More riders made it across to them as they neared the port city, including the Italian champion Costante Girardengo. Eventually eleven men sprinted for the win, with the previous year's winner, Philippe Thys, taking the honors. The small lead group contained a number of the other favorites, including Gustave Garrigou, Lapize, and Henri Pélissier. Faber and Petit-Breton had unfortunately both punctured, and they came in six minutes behind. It had taken the riders over thirteen hours to complete the stage.

It would be the next day before news of the assassination would break in France, but the story wasn't given much attention. The full impact of what had happened in Sarajevo would take weeks to be fully appreciated, not just in France, but everywhere else. British historian Zbynek Zeman would later write, "The event almost failed to make any impression whatsoever. On Sunday and Monday [June 28 and 29], the crowds in Vienna listened to music and drank wine, as if nothing had happened."

Yet in fact the assassination had started a chain of events that would lead to one of the most devastating conflicts ever just a little over a month later. At the war's onset, many of the cyclists competing in the Tour signed up. Fighting would drag on for much longer than anybody had envisaged and resulted in the deaths of millions of soldiers and civilians. Among those were many of the Tour cyclists.

1

The 1914 Tour

In July 1914, as the Tour went on and diplomatic negotiations were taking place throughout Europe, the French people were largely disinterested in events taking place in some distant countries. What was really capturing their attention was the sensational murder case of Henriette Caillaux. She was a Parisian socialite who had married Joseph Caillaux, a former minister of the interior. Earlier that year, on March 16, she was accused of shooting and killing the editor of the newspaper *Le Figaro*, Gaston Calmette. The reason given by the prosecution was that Calmette had received and published a letter belonging to her husband that had tarnished his reputation. The letter was in relation to the prime minister's rejection of a tax bill that he had publicly claimed to support.

Henriette believed that Calmette would publish more letters claiming that she had an affair with Joseph while he was still married to his first wife. Henriette decided to pay a visit to Calmette's office, where she shot him six times; he died six hours later. Events in Eastern

Europe couldn't compete for headlines with a scandalous court case like that. Henriette Caillaux would end up being acquitted two days after the Tour finished. However, the real significance of the shooting of Calmette would emerge later. Caillaux would have gone on to become prime minister but for the editor's murder, and it was widely believed that he could have averted war with Germany.

Unlike the Tour de France today, in 1914 the cyclists wouldn't race on consecutive days. The stages were so long that the riders would have had very limited rest if they were to finish one stage only to start the next the following morning. So it was two days after Archduke Franz Ferdinand's assassination that the riders lined up for their second stage from Le Havre to Cherbourg. On their rest day in Le Havre, the first newspaper reports of the assassination appeared. It didn't particularly interest those involved with the race, and even the president of the country, Raymond Poincaré, didn't seem particularly perturbed by the news. Indeed, Poincaré was at the horse racing track at Longchamp when the news broke, and such was his level of disinterest that he didn't even bother leaving. He was more concerned with watching Baron de Rothschild's horse Sardanapale winning the Grand Prix of Paris instead.

Having taken victory on the opening stage, Philippe Thys nearly repeated his win on the following stage to Cherbourg, but he was narrowly beaten by his compatriot Jean Rossius after the two had broken clear. Rossius had also finished with the group of eleven on the previous stage, so the two Belgians now shared the lead overall. There were significant time losses for some of the other big names on the stage, though: Lapize, Faber, Petit-Breton, and Eugène Christophe all lost big chunks of time. It was already starting to look like the Tour could be a two-horse race.

The third stage from Cherbourg to Brest got off to a bad start when the peloton took a wrong turn after four kilometers. Apparently a senior race official decided to leave one of his subordinates in charge; this man didn't really know what he was doing and sent the race the wrong way. It didn't help matters that in the darkness of night, the riders had been unable to see signposts. A car had to be sent after them to let them know of the mistake, and the commissaires decided to restart the stage in Coutances three hours later. It shortened the stage considerably.

It rained heavily that day, and toward the end thirteen riders broke clear. The stage was won by Emile Engel in what was by all accounts quite a dangerous sprint, but scandal would hit him a few stages later. It would end up a bittersweet race for Engel. Meanwhile there was no still no separating the Belgian duo of Thys and Rossius, who were more than seven minutes clear of the third-place man, Émile Georget.

Two days later the riders would take on the longest stage of the race, which was a mammoth 470 kilometers from Brest to La Rochelle. Two riders broke clear early on, Constant Ménager and

Georget, and stayed clear for much of the stage. Because he was sitting in third place overall going into the stage, Georget had a chance of taking over the lead if the pair worked together. With this in mind, Rossius's Alcyon team didn't give them too much free rein. Georget and Ménager were eventually caught. Coming toward La Rochelle, two riders broke clear from the pack, Henri Pélissier and Oscar Egg. They quickly claimed time on the rest, and at the finish Pélissier out-sprinted the Swiss man.

It was Pélissier's third attempt at the race, and despite not having finished a Tour, he was one of the riders fancied to take the overall victory. At that stage in his career, he had already won some very big one-day races, including Milan–San Remo and the Tour of Lombardy, as well as a stage of the previous year's Tour. However, he was also gaining a reputation for being particularly volatile and unpredictable, and that could be his undoing in the Tour. He had clawed back nearly two minutes on Rossius and Thys on the stage and was now just five minutes behind the leaders.

As the riders took a well-deserved rest by the Atlantic coast at La Rochelle, negotiations were heating up in Central and Eastern Europe. An Austrian foreign ministry official, Count Hoyos, had been dispatched to Berlin to ascertain the German position. He presented a letter from Emperor Franz Joseph of Austria to the German kaiser Wilhelm II outlining the strategy that the Austro-Hungarians felt they needed to take with their German allies to deal with the situation in the Balkans.

The kaiser, who was departing for a tour of Scandinavia, was still of the belief that neither Russia nor France would become engaged in any potential conflict. However, there were very close bilateral relations between Russia and Serbia, and the Russians were willing to defend their allies against attack.

If Russia were to become involved, then there was every likelihood that France would also. Relations between Germany and France had been extremely poor since the Franco-Prussian War, and, fearing the military strength of their neighbor, the French had started increasing the power of their armed forces. In 1894 they had also signed the Franco-Russian Alliance, which was a countermeasure to the development of the Triple Alliance among Germany, Austria-Hungary, and Italy. The Franco-Russian Alliance would become known as the Triple Entente after the signing of the Russian Entente with Great Britain in 1907. These agreements left the major countries of Europe primed for war.

The Tour de France continued south to Bayonne for the fifth stage. A previous holder of the world hour record, Oscar Egg, won his second consecutive stage as the race neared the Pyrénées. He was the fastest of the twenty-eight riders arriving together at the end of the 379 kilometers. There wasn't much change to the race standings, although one of the top riders did suffer that day: Italian champion Costante Girardengo crashed a number of times during the stage.

The conservative racing during that stage was quite possibly due to the riders wanting to keep their reserves for what was about to come, two consecutive stages through the Pyrénées. Desgrange wasn't happy with the way the stage had panned out, though: "The group crawled for 300 kilometers. It is now our fifth stage, and absolutely nothing happened at all."

The first Pyrenean stage went from Bayonne to Luchon, and it would see big time gaps emerging for the first time since the Tour started. What was fearful for the riders wasn't the length of the stage, but the climbs of the Col d'Aubisque, Col du Tourmalet, Col d'Aspin, and Col de Peyresourde. Girardengo crashed again on the stage; he had had enough, and pulled out of the race. Despite going on to win the Italian championships nine times in total, Milan–San Remo six times, the Tour of Lombardy three times, and the Giro d'Italia twice, he would never return to France to take part in the Tour.

Bad luck struck another individual that day. Ali Neffati from Tunisia was hit by one of the race official's cars on the Col d'Aubisque, and was unable to finish the stage. However, they ruled that he had been a victim of misfortune and allowed him to start the next stage. The Tunisian had made his debut in the race the year before, thereby becoming the first African to take part; he was also easily recognizable given that he raced in a fez. Neffati's debut had happened when other Tunisian sportsmen came together to raise enough money to send him to France. He would survive the forthcoming war, and would continue to race in both Europe and America until 1930.

Pélissier was aggressive again that day, attacking on the Col d'Aubisque along with Oscar Egg. By the top of the climb he had overcome his overall deficit on Thys. It was starting to look like a race-winning move, but the wheels would come off shortly afterward. Pélissier really started to struggle on the next climb, the Tourmalet. About three kilometers from the top, he started feeling light-headed. He had the hunger knock, whereby he was totally devoid of energy. Pélissier reached into his pockets for food, letting half of it drop on the ground, but it was too late. He tried to continue climbing but ended up collapsing onto the grass shoulder at the side of the road. Many of the other top favorites had passed him at this stage, including Thys. Pélissier ended up walking up the mountain. He started to come around somewhat on the descent, but on the next climb, the Aspin, the same thing happened: He collapsed at the side of the road.

This time Pélissier fell asleep on the grass and had to be revived by a teammate, Émile Georget. He continued to the end and managed to pass quite a few of the others along the way. However, despite still finishing in fourth, it seemed that his chance of overall victory was gone, as he was now more than half an hour behind Thys. Up front, the stage had been won by the Belgian Firmin Lambot, but—more important—Thys had gained significant time on everyone else, as Rossius finished nearly an hour behind.

Despite pressure from Henri Pélissier, Philippe Thys
hung on to win the 1914 Tour.

Two days later the riders would have more climbs to face on the next stage to Perpignan, which would go over the Col de Portet d'Aspet and Col de Puymorens. The stage was won by Jean Alavoine at the head of a small lead group that also contained Thys and Pélissier. All of the riders struggled that day in what was turning into a particularly hot summer in the south of France, and to a certain extent it was stifling the race. There were no significant changes to the General Classification. The high temperatures continued for the next stage, which was a transitional stage along the Mediterranean coastline to Marseille. Octave Lapize won his only stage of the race at the velodrome, and once again there were no General Classification changes. Despite having crashed near Arles, Thys continued to lead Pélissier by thirty-five minutes. The major talking point of the stage that day was the disqualification of Emile Engel for abusing a race official.

At this point there was a growing realization throughout Europe of the seriousness of the potential repercussions from the assassination of Archduke Franz Ferdinand. However, not everybody felt that war was inevitable. One man who was trying to stop France's seeming free fall toward warfare was the socialist politician Jean Jaurès. He was a staunch antimilitarist who spent much of July trying to prevent war. The previous year, Jaurès had opposed the extension of the French army draft period from one to three years.

Jaurès met with other socialist leaders from other countries, including Germany, Russia, and Britain, that month in Brussels to try to develop a solution that would prevent war. They proposed a general strike against the war. Unfortunately, despite high levels of support, the race toward war was rapid, and in France there was an incredible amount of passion about regaining the provinces of Alsace and Lorraine, which had been annexed by Germany.

On his return to Paris, Jaurès was tragically shot and killed in a café in Montmartre by twenty-nine-year-old French nationalist Raoul Villain on July 31. Any slim hope of avoiding war now seemed to have been extinguished. The French winner of the Nobel Prize for Literature, Romain Rolland, was to later say of Jaurès, "If he had lived, he alone could have stopped this misery."

Down south the heat was incessant, and along the way to Nice on Bastille Day the peloton decided to cease hostilities and try to cool down. They stopped along the coast and jumped into the Mediterranean. When the race arrived in Nice, the riders had a lap to do before finishing, which included the climb at La Turbie. It looked like Maurice Brocco from the Gladiator-Dunlop team would take the stage win until he hit the climb and had to resort to walking. He was passed by Jean Rossius, who went on to win the stage, and moved into third place overall. Pélissier and Thys were inseparable again, finishing together seven minutes behind Rossius. There was misfortune for another rider on La Turbie that day as the Alcyon team leader Marcel Buysse ended up in hospital after hitting a motorcyclist on the descent.

Other riders also struggled that day. The 1912 winner, Odile Defraye, lost more than four hours, and Paul Deman and Lucien Petit-Breton were among those who abandoned. Upon arriving in Nice, Petit-Breton had received the sad news that his mother had died, and he subsequently pulled out of the race.

The race would head north toward the Alps on the next stage, and the riders would have a number of climbs to contend with on their way to Grenoble. There were more crashes that day as Jean Alavoine and Jean Rossius collided on the Col de la Colle-Saint-Michel. They were distanced by many of the other big riders, and tried to chase back. Alavoine made it, but Rossius struggled. The lead group was reduced to just four riders going over the final climb of the day, the 1,246-meter-high Col Bayard, and Pélissier was fastest in the sprint to claim his first stage win of that year's race. He couldn't gain any time on Thys, though, as he was also in the four-man group with Firmin Lambot and Jean Alavoine.

The next stage was one of the most difficult of the race: Riders would have to negotiate the Col du Lauteret, the Col du Galibier, and the Col des Aravis. Despite Pélissier having to dismount on the Galibier a number of times, Thys was unable to shake him. Only one other man was able to stay with the leading duo, their Peugeot teammate, Gustave Garrigou. It was an amazing ride by Garrigou, who had crashed on the descent of the Aravis then punctured in Annecy; he only caught the leading two with seven kilometers remaining. He still had enough strength though to outsprint the other two at the finish in Geneva for his eighth and final-ever stage win of the Tour. The start of the war would signal the end of his career, as he wouldn't continue racing after the cessation of hostilities.

In the 1914 Tour many of the riders were still using two-sided rear hubs, whereby they would have to dismount and flip their wheels around to change gears. This would cause the race leader, Thys, some problems on the twelfth stage to Belfort. There was still a large leading group of thirty-three riders as they reached the foot of the final climb that day, the Ballon d'Alsace. The riders dismounted at the bottom to change gears, but for some reason Thys had a problem refitting his back wheel; he was a few minutes behind the rest when he finally got going. Pélissier and Alavoine took advantage and pressed on, and it looked like it would be a sprint between the two for the stage win. However, Alavoine punctured close to the finish, enabling Pélissier to take his second stage win. In the end Thys lost only two and a half minutes to the second-place man that day, so he still maintained a comfortable lead with just three stages remaining.

On the same day that Pélissier was winning in Belfort, the French president, Raymond Poincaré, was starting his visit to St. Petersburg to meet with Russian leaders and discuss the increasing Austro-Serbian tension and the ever-increasing threat of war. During the series of meetings, Poincaré assured the Russians that if a conflict broke out over the Serbian issue, the Russians would have the full support of the French. Some historians have suggested that Poincaré had an opportunity to use this conference to try to restrain the Russians rather being so up front in support. The French ambassador to Russia in 1914, Maurice Paléologue, later wrote that the French were not concerned that they would be dragged into the war by Russia, but rather that France would be "poorly supported by Russia, in the event of a German attack." The chances of averting war appeared to be getting slimmer and slimmer.

The Tour de France was entering its last few days, and it was looking good for Thys. On the thirteenth stage from Belfort to Longwy the 1909 Tour winner, François Faber, attacked alone after 114 kilometers. It was a long way to the finish for one man, but he pressed on regardless. Although he was in tenth position on General Classification, Faber was nearly seven hours behind Thys so he was no threat to his overall lead. Faber looked comfortable for taking the stage win. In the state of heightened political tension, the army's presence was becoming more noticeable: On Faber's breakaway, he was accompanied by a soldier from one of the cycling units.

Faber really struggled in the last hour of his breakaway, though. Desgrange reported that he started "zigzagging somewhat." However, it seems that it wasn't just fatigue that was affecting Faber's ability to cycle in a straight line; he may have taken something that was causing his unsteadiness. He struggled on, but with ten kilometers remaining he ended up colliding with a car. He regained his feet and pushed on. Despite his fall, he was able to stay away from his pursuers to win the stage from Pélissier by more than six minutes. A reporter wrote afterward, "All those who saw Faber's arrival were stunned by the level of his drunkenness." For many years it would be common practice for cyclists to numb their pain with alcohol, but it seemed that Faber may have taken it a bit too far. Once again, there was nothing to separate Thys and Pélissier at the finish.

A notable top ten finisher that day was the Australian Donald Kirkham, who ended up in ninth place. Kirkham, along with fellow Aussie Iddo Munro, was riding for the Phebus-Dunlop team. They had traveled over to Europe at the start of the year, and had been joined on the trip by four other compatriots. The Australians took part in many of the big classic races that spring, including Paris–Roubaix and Milan–San Remo, but only Munro and Kirkham would make it to the Tour.

For some reason the two Australians were dubbed "the cannibals" by the French press, and they did have to put up with some problems from the rest of the peloton during the race, particularly on the stage from Marseille to Nice. At one stage they considered quitting—such was the level of abuse that they received—but they were persuaded to stay in by the race organizers. Both would go on to finish.

On July 23, as the Tour riders were resting in Longwy, Baron Giesl von Gieslingen, ambassador of the Austro-Hungarian Empire to Serbia, delivered an ultimatum to the Serbian foreign ministry. The intention of the Austro-Hungarians was to initiate a conflict that would result in the rapid defeat of Serbia before the rest of Europe even had time to react. The ultimatum put various demands on Serbia, such as repressing all anti-Austrian propaganda and the elimination of all terrorist groups, including the Black Hand organization. The Austrians demanded an answer within forty-eight hours.

Upon receipt of the ultimatum, the Serbians corresponded with the Russian government. The Russian foreign minister outlined his opinion that the archduke's death was being used as a pretext for war by the Germans and Austrians. The Russians said that they would start preparing their troops for mobilization, which was not what had been predicted by the German government. The Serbians responded to the Austrians just before the deadline, confirming that they would meet all of Austria's demands except one. They could not agree to Austria-Hungary being involved in an internal inquiry into the assassination. The response resulted in Austria-Hungary breaking off diplomatic relations with Serbia.

The penultimate stage of the Tour took place the day after the Austro-Hungarians had delivered their ultimatum. The stage would take the riders from Longwy to Dunkirk. François Faber won his second stage in a row, finishing in the same time as Henri Pélissier and Philippe Thys. However, despite Pélissier not being able to break clear of the Belgian, his deficit had been reduced from nearly thirty-two minutes to just one minute and fifty seconds. The commissaires had penalized Thys by thirty minutes for breaking the rules.

He had collided with Faber during the stage and broken a wheel when he fell. He chose to buy a new one, rather than try to repair it. The rules stated that a rider had to repair any mechanical issues himself without any outside help. Alternatively, if a race commissaire deemed it to be irreparable, he could get assistance. Thys knew he would receive a thirty-minute penalty, but he gambled that it would take him longer to make the repair. It was all set up for a fight to the finish on the final stage.

Little did either the spectators or the cyclists know prior to the final stage that this would be the last Tour de France action that would be seen for nearly five years. The riders signed on that morning in the Café des Arcades in Dunkirk before setting off on the 340-kilometer stage to Paris.

Pélissier did his very best to break away from Thys that day, but to no avail. The weather didn't favor Pélissier, either, as the peloton would have to face a really strong headwind on the road to Paris. A headwind tends to favor the bunch rather than those trying for a breakaway attempt, and as a result the bunch would stay together for much of the stage. Pélissier would have to bide his time.

To the west of Paris, at Marly-le-Roi, Pélissier finally attacked and gave it his all. It was now or never. He set a ferocious pace, and it was starting to look like he could overcome his deficit. However, it all went wrong for him at the bridge at Saint-Cloud to the west of Paris.

A sizable number of his supporters had gathered on the bridge, and as they tried to cheer and push their man to victory, they ended up impeding his progress. It was incredibly frustrating for the Frenchman seeing his chance at victory slipping away.

Pélissier described the scene afterward: "The rows of spectators narrowed, leaving me with just a small gap. They cheered me as if I had won, and they are trying to make me lose. I had to dismount. I cried in desperation, but my voice was lost."

He was soon caught by three others, including Thys. His chance at glory had disappeared. It would be of little consolation to him that he was still strong enough to take the final stage win. He had lost by just one minute and fifty seconds, which would remain the smallest margin between first and second for over forty years. Thys meanwhile, at the age of just twenty-four, had become the second rider after Lucien Petit-Breton to win the race twice. The future looked bright for the man from Anderlecht, and in one of the best team performances ever seen at the Tour, the Peugeot team won twelve of the fifteen stages and placed ten riders in the top thirteen.

Two days after the end of the Tour, the Austro-Hungarian Empire declared war on Serbia. In the last few desperate bids to avert the conflict, Great Britain tried to establish international mediation and the Russians urged German restraint. However, in a defensive measure, the Russians began to mobilize their troops, which in turn resulted in the Germans also mobilizing their army. Within days, the war would start.

Jean Alavoine en route to winning Stage 7.

Stage 8 final sprint with Maurice Brocco ahead of Octave Lapize,
Oscar Egg, and Emile Engel, just prior to the crash that led to
Engel's ejection from the Tour.

2

A Call to Arms

On August 2 German soldiers crossed the French border for the first time since the Franco-Prussian War in 1871, and upon hearing the news French troops rushed to intercept them. Their first engagement was at Joncherey, twenty kilometers south of Belfort and close to the Swiss border, and at that clash a French soldier was shot dead. Corporal Jules André Peugeot had become the first French victim of the war, which would go on to claim millions of lives. A memorial now marks the spot, which reads, "On Sunday 2 August 1914 Corporal Jules André Peugeot of the 44e R.I. was killed here during a mission at a border post at Joncherey. More than 30 hours before she declared war to France, Imperial Germany has already spilled the first French blood of the War of 1914–1918."

The following afternoon, and two days after declaring war on Russia, Germany declared war on France. Hours later France would make its own declaration of war against Germany, with the intention of moving troops into the regions of Alsace and Lorraine, which it had lost in the Franco-Prussian War in 1871. The signing of the Treaty of Frankfurt at the end of that war had resulted in the relinquishing of nearly seventeen hundred villages, towns, and cities in those regions to Germany. The loss of these areas would influence French politics over the next forty years. Georges Clemenceau, who would go on to become French prime minister during the war, felt that the country needed to divert attention away from the scramble for Africa and instead concentrate on reclaiming the lost territories. It would also become one of the primary motivations for France to take up arms against its neighbor.

That same day as the declaration of war, Tour organizer Henri Desgrange published an amazing article printed in red ink, in *L'Auto*, asking his countrymen to join the fight. He didn't hold back in displaying his vitriolic attitude toward the Germans, making references to a battle from the Franco-Prussian War, and also an earlier battle from the Napoleonic era. Desgrange used a sporting reference for the article title, which was titled "Le Grand Match" (The Big Match):

My little fellas, my darling little fellas, my little French fellas. Listen to me carefully. In the 14 years L'Auto *has been published, every day, it has never given you wrong advice, has it? So listen to me. The Prussians are bastards. I use this word, not to mean "lucky," but in its literal sense. And I talk about*

Prussians, not to be mistaken with Germans, it is because I do not believe that all German brains have been melted into the German mold. See for yourself those square heads; stupid sheep, not showing any initiative, only good for the butcher.

My little fellas, my darling little fellas, my little French fellas. Listen to me, listen to me carefully. You have to go and get those bastards. Believe it. It is impossible for a French man to fall in front of what is a German man. It is a big match to fight: use all your tricks. You know all that, my little fellas, more than I do myself, me, who has been teaching it for nearly 15 years.

But watch out. When your rifle butt will be on their chest, they will ask you for forgiveness. Don't let them trick you. Pull the trigger without pity, and when you will have really pulled the trigger, and you will have eliminated as many as is necessary, then, we'll see. But out of the 5 liters of blood that their carcasses holds, let at least 4 flow, and you will see that when they are down to 1 liter per man, they will understand that Alsace and Lorraine are French territories. We have to get rid of those evil imbeciles who, for the last 4 years, are keeping us from loving, from breathing and from being happy.

 Ah! What a sigh will humanity breathe, my little fellas, if you are victorious. How we will breathe. How we'll find life good and beautiful! And then, no more grotesques, no more "sauerkrautmen," no more clock thieves, no more zinc imperators who fix their mustaches while declaring that Germany is being "attacked." No more Kaiser, no more Agadir, no more blood tax. No more nightmares, no more bastards.

 It's all down to you, my little fellas, my darling little fellas, my little French fellas. We have had the first round at Jena, they had the second at Sedan. To us, victory, if you want it like the French know how to want when they want!

It wasn't only *L'Auto* that was publishing such articles. On August 4 another newspaper, *Le Matin,* called the war a "holy war of civilization against barbarity." It's unknown whether Desgrange's call to arms was the reason so many of the Tour de France cyclists signed up; regardless, many would tragically die in those first few months. Desgrange himself would become involved as at the start of the war, establishing the Comité d'éducation physique de Paris, at the École Spéciale Militaire de Saint-Cyr, which had the aim of advancing the physical education of soldiers.

Desgrange wasn't just a journalist; he also had extensive experience in the area of athletics. In the 1890s he had been a very accomplished cyclist himself, setting the world hour record among other achievements. The defeat to the Prussians occurred when he was just a child. It was something that had really gnawed at him, and he put the blame on the superior fitness of the enemy forces. Prior to the war he had written about the weakness of the younger French generation, describing them as "tired, without muscle, without character and without willpower." Desgrange would go on to help train thousands of soldiers, believing that an increase in overall fitness of the French army would be the primary reason they would defeat their enemy.

Three years later in April 1917, and despite being fifty years old at the time, Desgrange himself would sign up for the army. He would serve the last two years of the conflict with the Nineteenth Infantry Regiment, based in Autun in the Saône-et-Loire department, and he spent some time at the front. His efforts saw him receive the French Croix de Guerre military honor. Desgrange also somehow managed to find time to continue to write for *L'Auto* throughout the war. He would be released from service in January 1919, enabling him to concentrate on the organization of the Tour de France again.

Along with the famous cyclists who had joined the fight, many other French sportsmen would also take up arms. Among the most recognizable names was Roland Garros. Not only was Garros one of the most famous French aviators at that time and the developer of

The founder of the Tour de France, Henri Desgrange,
would write a stirring article at the start of the war
urging his countrymen to join the fight.

the tractor propeller for fighter planes, but he had also taken part in
and been successful in many sports, including tennis and cycling. In
1896 he had won the French university cycling championships.

Jean Bouin, an athletics star and a silver medalist for France in the
1912 Olympics in Stockholm in the 5000 meters, was killed in action
in September 1914. The stadium of the rugby team, Stade Français,
would be named in his honor.

Another famous French sportsman, Henri Decoin, who had competed in swimming in the 1908 Olympics and water polo in the 1912
Olympics, would make a comparison between war and sport that
somewhat echoed Desgrange's call to arms. In an interview in *L'Auto*

in 1916, Decoin said, "Who said the Olympic Games of 1916 would not take place? Let us look at what is happening: the Olympic Games, the real games, the great games are taking place at the moment with intense fury. The nations have poured the cream of their race into the arena for the final victory." Decoin would survive the war and go on to become a well-known film director.

It wasn't only sportsmen from France who took up the fight. Numerous footballers, rugby players, Australian Rules players, hockey players, cricketers, boxers, and other athletes from Britain, Ireland, Australia, New Zealand, and elsewhere would become involved; in some cases entire teams were decimated. Men who had played together on the same team would often sign up alongside one another for the same regiment.

Three weeks after the start of the war, the first British soldier was killed, and he would happen to be a cyclist. John Parr was a member of the Divisional Mounted Troops, Third Company, Army Cyclists, and he was part of a bicycle reconnaissance unit near Oburg, just north of Mons. The exact details of his death are unclear, but he and a comrade encountered a patrol from the German First Army. The other soldier cycled back to report the sighting; when he returned, Parr had been shot dead.

His grave stated that he was twenty years old when he was killed, but he was in fact just sixteen. He had lied about his age when enlisting. The British weren't the only army to form cycling units during the war—the French, Italians, and Germans did also—but ironically enough, it doesn't appear that many of the Tour de France cyclists were appointed to these units.

In an effort to match the strength of Germany's army, France introduced a "Three Year Law" in 1913. The law required all healthy men from the age of twenty to undertake three years of military service, rather than the previous one year. At the start of the war, in August 1914, 2.9 million French men were mobilized, including conscripts undertaking their three years of service, army reservists who had already completed their service, and also members of the territorial army.

In France, and in other countries, there was much initial enthusiasm among those who were the first to sign up. It was seen as being a great adventure. That enthusiasm wouldn't last, as there were massive casualties from the start. In that first month alone, hundreds of thousands of soldiers were killed and injured.

One of the first cyclists to die in action, Philippe Cordier, was killed within weeks of the declaration of war. Cordier was born on June 17, 1888, in Narbonne and had raced with the Griffon-Wolber team in 1909. He took part in that year's Tour but didn't finish. He died less than three weeks after the start of the war, on August 22 at Luneville at the Battle of the Frontiers. Erroneous reports would also emerge in the first few months of the war about the fate of a number of other Tour cyclists. A report that appeared early on in the war in

British and Australian newspapers read as follows:

> *Philippe Thys, the Belgian crack road rider winner of the last Tour de France race in July, has been killed. The competitors, after having ridden Le Havre, Cherbourg, Brest, Bayonne, Marseilles, Nice, Geneva, Belfort, Longwy and Dunkirk, arrived back in Paris on July the 20th. A week later war was declared. Thys and the brothers Buysse—Marcel and Lucien— went to fight for their country, Belgium. All three are now dead. The French riders, Francois Faber and Louis Trousselier have also been killed: Comès, the cyclist sprinter, is reported to be wounded.*

It was a reflection of the fog of war that existed that not one of the six cyclists listed was actually dead at that time. Lucien Buysse, in fact, would live to the ripe old age of eighty-seven. Despite the mistaken report, unfortunately, it wouldn't take long until more casualties from the cycling world would emerge.

A crash at the finish of a stage.

The top riders at the 1914 Tour all drank "Koto wine containing
Peruvian coca," according to an advertorial that appeared in *L'Auto*.

3

The Rape of Belgium

Just over a week after the start of hostilities, the cycling world would experience its first casualty when one of the top Belgian cyclists was mercilessly killed. Marcel Kerff hadn't taken part in the Tour that had finished the previous week—his career was long since over—but he had competed in the very first running of the race back in 1903.

Kerff was living close to the German border when the invasion began on August 4. At just after 8 AM the German First, Second, and Third Armies started crossing the border. Their intention was to first capture Liège, and then move quickly through Belgium and into northern France. The previous week the British government had made a request to Germany that Belgium's neutrality be respected. On the same day that Belgium was invaded, Britain declared war on Germany.

The previous decade German field marshal Count Alfred von Schlieffen had developed a plan in the event that the German Empire would find itself fighting on fronts in both the east and the west. An element of the strategy that would become known as the Schlieffen Plan involved Germany invading Belgium before attacking France, and so on August 2, the German government demanded that their army be given access through Belgium, but they were refused passage.

Belgium had a fighting force of just 117,000 troops and should have been no match for the Germans. Despite their limited numbers, however, the Belgians put up considerable resistance. It would be two weeks before the Germans would capture Liège, but Namur and Brussels would fall soon after. One of the initial areas that the invaders would overrun was the region where Kerff was from.

Kerff was born in the Flandrian village of Sint-Martens-Voeren in 1866, which is beside the border with the French-speaking Walloon region. The village is also just a few hundred meters from the Dutch border, and less than twenty kilometers from Germany. He was from a family of ten boys, and two of his brothers, Leopold and Charles, would also race as professional cyclists. Their father was a butcher who often asked his sons to cycle to Paris to purchase meat from wholesalers. The round trip was an incredible seven hundred kilometers for the boys, and the return involved hauling large pieces of meat, but the boys loved the freedom that they were given.

Bicycle racing was in its infancy in Belgium when Marcel turned professional in 1896. The advent of the sport was a little late for him, though, as he was already thirty years old when he started racing professionally. A race that he adapted to quickly was Paris–Roubaix, which had its first running that year. In the second edition of the race, Marcel finished in tenth place, and he would finish in sixth place in 1899. Despite some good results, though, he didn't manage to win a race until 1900. In that year he took victory in the forty-eight hours of Antwerp race, and finished third in the twenty-four hours of Verviers.

The following year he came close to winning some more big races, as he finished in second place in both the twenty-four hours of Antwerp and the twenty-four hours of Verviers. He also came second in the first edition of Brussels–Roubaix, behind the brilliantly named Hippolyte Aucouturier. Aucouturier, like Kerff, would also excel in Paris–Roubaix, in addition to finishing in second place in the 1905 Tour de France.

Kerff's brothers had differing fortunes in the sport. Leopold, who was fifteen years Marcel's junior, had very limited success: His third place in the twenty-four hours of Verviers of 1899 was his best result, and his career was short-lived. Charles was considerably more successful.

Charles won the Belgian Derny Championships in 1901, and would also finish in third place in the twenty-four hours of Verviers that year, meaning that for three years in a row a different Kerff brother finished in third place in the same race. Charles also traveled across the Atlantic that same year to take part in the New York Six-Day.

Unfortunately for the Kerff family, tragedy struck in 1902. That May, Marcel and Charles entered the inaugural Marseille–Paris stage race, alongside thirteen others. The 920-kilometer race, which was run over two stages, was held in appalling conditions. On the first stage in torrential rain, Charles crashed heavily into a pile of stones at Aix-en-Provence and suffered a traumatic chest injury. He was rushed to the nearby hospital, but died just a few minutes after he was admitted.

Marcel raced on without knowing what had happened to his brother, and somehow the news was even kept from him overnight, before the riders started the second stage to Paris. He finished in fourth place overall at the end of the race in Parc des Princes, where the news was finally broken to him. He was understandably distraught. Soon after the incident rumors started circulating that the tragedy had not been an accident. It was said that the younger Kerff brother had actually been pulled off his bike and beaten up by angry French supporters who didn't want to see him move into the lead.

This story isn't entirely implausible; it wasn't unknown at that time for riders to be attacked by overzealous fans. In the infamous 1904 Tour de France, for example, there were numerous incidents of riders being assaulted. Maurice Garin and Lucien Pothier were attacked by four masked men in a car on the first stage. Rocks were thrown at riders on the third stage, and nails were thrown on the road during some of the other stages. Such was the scale of the problems during the race that the organizers considered canceling the Tour. The truth of Charles Kerff's untimely death in Marseille–Paris has never been established.

Despite the tragic death of his brother, Marcel continued racing. The following year he signed up to start the inaugural Tour de France. He, along with the fifty-nine other riders, would have to face six stages totaling 2,428 kilometers.

On the first stage to Lyon, he finished in sixth place, an hour and forty-two minutes behind the winner Maurice Garin, who won in a time of seventeen hours and forty-five minutes. The yellow jersey had not yet been thought of, so Garin was given a green armband to denote that he was the leader of the race. Only thirty-seven riders managed to finish the stage, with the first riders abandoning just fifty kilometers in. However, those who abandoned were allowed to start subsequent stages. It just meant that they wouldn't be included in the General Classification.

On the second stage four days later, from Lyon to Marseille, Kerff suffered terribly in the heat of the Rhône Valley. His thirst was so great that he even resorted to drinking from a bucket of dirty water that other riders had been using to wash themselves. The riders also had to negotiate the first-ever climb in the race, the 1,161-meter Col de la République near Saint-Etienne. Despite his suffering, Kerff finished in seventh place on the stage.

Three days later the riders faced a stage of 423 kilometers from Marseille to Toulouse. Hippolyte Aucouturier won the stage, while Marcel finished more than an hour and a half behind. Unlike others in the race who had a considerable amount of support, Kerff had no team behind him and had to fend for himself throughout the race. After each stage he had to go in search of food and lodgings for the night. He also had to look after his own bike and make any repairs it needed. It had been bought for him a few years previously by friends.

On the fourth stage from Toulouse to Bordeaux, he suffered from multiple punctures but refused to give up. The penultimate stage, which they faced the very next day, took the riders 425 kilometers to Nantes. At one point Kerff was so famished that he stole a loaf of bread, which he then shared with other riders, including Frenchman Jean Dargassies and German Josef Fischer.

Kerff eventually finished in sixth place overall at the end of the race in Paris, nearly six hours behind the winner, Maurice Garin. The top five had all been members of the mighty La Française team. Kerff had proved to be the best of the rest as well as being the top Belgian, finishing one place ahead of his compatriot Julien Lootens, and four places ahead of Alois Catteau. Only twenty-one riders made it to Paris, the last of whom, Arsène Millocheau, was more than sixty-four hours behind Garin.

Maurice Garin became a national hero, and his winning margin of two hours and forty-nine minutes is still the biggest in the history of the race. Desgrange would later acclaim the achievement of the riders in finishing the race: "The steepest mountains, the coldest and blackest nights, the sharpest and most violent winds, the most difficult routes, never-ending slopes and roads that just keep going on and on—nothing has been able to break the willpower and determination of these men."

Kerff's sixth place in that Tour de France was his last big result, and he retired the following year at the age of thirty-seven. He returned to Sint-Martens-Voeren and continued to help out in the family butcher business; he would also gain employment as a butler and driver at Teuven Kasteel, the large castle in a neighboring village.

He was still living in Sint-Martens-Voeren when the war started the following decade. In the days following the start of the invasion, some units of the German army were encamped near Moelingen when curiosity got the better of Kerff; along with some friends he decided to hop on his bicycle and go and have a look at the invading forces. He wasn't alone—on the day that the invasion had started, thousands of curious onlookers had traveled to the village of Mesch, just across the Dutch border, to witness the firepower of the Germans.

When he set off to have a look at what was happening in Moelingen, there were already twenty-five thousand Germans camped in the border region. Kerff was spotted, and unfortunately the Germans didn't see his presence there as mere curiosity. They arrested him on charges of espionage.

He tried to protest his innocence, to no avail. When called for help from nearby residents, the Germans were reported to have cut out his tongue. The friends of Kerff's were also arrested and would also be charged with espionage. On August 7 Kerff was sentenced to death. He and five other men from the locality were hanged from a tree. Another six men were shot on charges of spying.

His and the others' bodies wouldn't be found until a year later, when a mass grave was uncovered beside the main road at Moelingen. The execution of Marcel and the others was not an isolated incident, however. In what became known as the Rape of Belgium, the Germans committed numerous atrocities during the opening months of the war. The war crimes had started almost immediately, when the Germans encountered resistance at Visé, just a few kilometers east of Marcel's home.

There they found that Belgian troops had blown up the bridge over the Meuse to slow their advance, and they were being shot at from across the river. The Germans accused the locals of having helped the Belgian troops and started to take their revenge. They burned houses, shot and bayoneted villagers, and tore apart houses looking for concealed weapons.

Within just a few days of the invasion, hundreds of civilians had

In 1933, a memorial was laid at the spot where
Marcel Kerff and his friends were killed.

been killed by the Germans. There were numerous incidents of executions in Andenne, Dinant, Aarschot, and Tamines. On August 25, in one of the more massive atrocities, the German army laid siege to Leuven, burning the library and its collection of three hundred thousand books, killing 248 residents and expelling another 10,000 civilians. In Brabant, German soldiers had ordered a group of nuns to strip naked, fearing that they were spies. It was felt by many that the actions of the Germans were fueled by the resistance of the Belgians, which they hadn't foreseen.

It was estimated that by the end of the atrocities, six thousand Belgians had been killed, twenty-five thousand buildings had been destroyed, and over one and a half million residents were forced to flee their houses. The occupying authorities shipped money from the vaults of Belgian banks back to Germany. More than half of the cattle and pigs in the country and machinery from its factories were seized by the Germans.

In addition to the widespread executions, twenty thousand Belgians were forcibly transported to Germany to work in factories, and Belgian industry was used for war production by the Germans. Prior to the war, Belgium had been ranked the sixth most industrialized country in the world; this was the start of a slide from which it would never recover.

Kerff's home village, Sint-Martens-Voeren, was largely destroyed during the first year of the war, and had to be rebuilt afterward. A memorial was later built to commemorate him and all the other Belgian cyclists who would be killed in World War One. The monument is in Moelingen, not far from his home village and close to the spot where Marcel was killed. It sits near the route of the Amstel Gold race, and despite the passage of time, his engraved name is still clearly visible.

During the 1995 Tour de France, which had a stage finish in nearby Liège, the race organizers visited the memorial to pay their respects to the first and oldest Tour cyclist to be killed in the First World War. Unfortunately cycling would see more victims very soon afterward.

4

A Clash with Desgrange

The early years of the Tour de France would see many clashes between the organizers and the riders, usually as a result of the incredibly difficult conditions that the cyclists had to contend with, but there was typically only one winner in these disagreements: Henri Desgrange.

One man who crossed paths with Desgrange was Emile Engel, who was disqualified after Stage 8 of the 1914 Tour. For Engel it was an incredibly disappointing end to a race in which he had already won a stage. Unfortunately he wouldn't get another opportunity to take part in the Tour.

Engel was born in 1889 in Colombes, a northwestern suburb of Paris. It was the same town that the 1909 Tour winner François Faber hailed from, and the two would go on to become firm friends. Engel started racing professionally at the age of twenty-one as an *isolé* in 1910, and he had his first big win that year in the *Indépendents* class of the Tour de France. He was first across the line in the tenth stage to La Rochelle. More impressively, though, that season he also finished third in Paris–Tours behind Faber and Louis Trousselier. The following year he would win another stage of the Tour de France des Indépendents, and this result was enough to see him being signed by the top team at the time, Peugeot-Wolber. Among his new teammates were Lucien Petit-Breton, Oscar Egg, and Philippe Thys.

His older brother Louis would turn professional two years after Emile. Louis was second in the French championships in 1912 behind Octave Lapize, and also finished in fifteenth place in that year's Tour. Louis competed again in the Tour in 1914, finishing in forty-second place.

Emile had an underwhelming first season with his new team, but in 1913 he really came to prominence when he won the opening stage of the Tour of Belgium. Later in the season he managed a second place on the final stage of the Tour de France behind Marcel Buysse, and ended up in tenth place overall. Like many other top cyclists of the time, during the winter Engel would take part in track races, often partnering Faber, and they achieved a decent amount of success. The twenty-four-year-old was growing from strength to strength.

The 1914 season would be Engel's best to date. That spring he was second in both Paris–Menin behind Philippe Thys and Paris–Tours behind Oscar Egg, and a big win seemed inevitable. It nearly

Emile Engel and François Faber were both from Colombes,
and would become good friends.

came in the French championships at Versailles, but once again he would occupy the runner-up spot, this time behind Charles Crupelandt.

The 1914 Tour started off well for Engel, as he claimed a third place on the second stage from Le Havre to Cherbourg. He finished alone; two of the strongest riders in the race, Philippe Thys and Jean Rossius, had broken away earlier to fight out the stage win. It augured well for Engel that he was in such good form. On the next stage, to Brest, he managed to get into the small lead group coming toward the finish, which also contained riders of the class of Thys, Lucien Petit-Breton, and Octave Lapize. Engel knew his form was good, though, and he wasn't afraid of anyone. He was reported to have used his elbows to force his way to the front, but he was able to outsprint everyone at the end of the 405 kilometers to take the win. It would be his first and only Tour stage win.

Unfortunately for Engel, the Tour would end on a sour note. On the stage to Marseille, he was disqualified. That stage was run off in incredible heat, and there didn't seem to be much enthusiasm for racing. This resulted in twenty-five riders arriving together at the velodrome in Marseille to fight out the finish. The organizers felt that this was too many to contest the sprint on the track, so they decided to run a series of knockout races, then two semifinals with four riders in each, culminating in a final among four qualifiers.

The four riders who ended up qualifying for the final were Engel,

Octave Lapize, Maurice Brocco, and Oscar Egg. It was said to have been quite a scrappy race with a lot of contact. Coming into the last bend, Engel, Egg, and Lapize clashed, and Engel ended up falling. He was absolutely livid at the finish. He lodged an official complaint, which was dismissed by the commissaires. Engel was enraged when he heard this and started verbally and physically abusing an official. Fighting with a commissaire was not something that Desgrange would tolerate, and he decided to disqualify Engel from the race. Desgrange would later say that such violence was "the worst offense a racer can commit, because it relates to the principles of authority." It was the last race that Engel would ever take part in. After the Tour, Engel had been contracted to take part in a track race at the Vélodrome Buffalo in Paris, but it was canceled.

Desgrange wrote about the dismissal of Engel and suggested that the young rider was thoroughly remorseful for his behavior. He said that Engel had "asked Baugé (his team manager) to express his regrets for what he had done [and] promised him to be calmer in the future. Baugé and Engel then embraced with tears in their eyes. Engel! Now that's very good."

Writer Christopher S. Thompson, suggested in his book *The Tour de France: A Cultural History* that this scene may have even been fabricated by Desgrange to demonstrate to potential sponsors and critics of the race that cyclists who stood up to the race officials would humbly accept their punishment and be totally remorseful for their

Emile Engel fell foul of Henri Desgrange at the 1914 Tour.

wrongdoings. Desgrange would also infer that Engel's and others' insolence was due to their working-class backgrounds. He wrote in the days after Engel's expulsion,

> *Almost all of [the racers are] from humble origins, their existence is completely turned upside down one day solely because of their muscular power; they are offered small fortunes, they are showered with attention, their whims are obeyed, and they gradually get to the point where they forget even the essential principle that sport, on which they depend for a living, itself depends solely on discipline. When that happens everything goes wrong, and if you left them to themselves and to their whims, they would lose their jobs.*

Throughout his tenure as director of the Tour de France, Desgrange never changed his managerial stance, which the renowned *L'Équipe* journalist Pierre Chany would later write about. He said, "He knew the imperfections of his work, which was still in progress, but it was as if he didn't see them. He rejected advice, certain of his authority and decisions, powerful in a world where his word had the force of law. He followed a narrow path between the interests of cycling in general and his own, a way of thinking that justified his reputation as a despot."

Engel did have the consolation of seeing his teammate Philippe

Thys taking the final victory in Paris. The following week Engel signed up to fight for his country as soon as war was declared. He was assigned to the Seventy-Second Infantry, which was mobilized on August 2. The regiment, commanded by Colonel Toulorge, departed Amiens by train three days later, disembarking at Dun-sur-Meuse thirty kilometers north of Verdun. They saw combat almost immediately in Belgium in the Battle of the Frontiers, which was actually a series of battles along the French-Belgian border.

Engel would be involved in one of the first clashes between German and French troops at Virton, the southernmost town in Belgium, between August 22 and 24. The German army summarily executed hundreds of inhabitants of the town on the first day of that battle. Engel's regiment struggled over those few days of fighting and was given the order to retreat on August 24, along with the rest of the French army and the British Expeditionary Force (BEF). French losses in that first month of the war were massive, with 75,000 dead and total casualties of 260,000.

Coming into the war, the French were seriously handicapped by the outdated plan that had been developed the previous year. Plan XVII, which outlined the strategy for the offensive on Alsace-Lorraine, was based on attacks using cavalry charges and advances by infantry with fixed bayonets. The French army's naïveté with regard to modern warfare was also shown at the Battle of the Frontiers: Troops still wore the old uniforms of blue coats and bright red trousers.

When a politician had questioned the minister for war, Eugene Etienne, on the appropriateness of the uniform, he was shouted down: *"Le pantalon rouge c'est la France!"* Zouave troops from North African colonies would wear red caps with baggy white trousers, and cavalrymen wore feathered tall brass helmets. The French army would eventually relinquish their colorful garb and adopt a grayish-blue uniform instead.

Although they had been forced into retreat by the strength of the three invading German armies, the French and British rear-guard actions did help to delay the German advance. This action, in turn, gave the French time to transfer their forces to the west to defend Paris. This resulted in the First Battle of the Marne, fought between September 5 and 12.

At the start of the battle, Marshal Joseph Joffre, the commander in chief of the French army, issued a rousing order to French troops declaring that the fate of the country was at stake, that soldiers must be prepared to die rather than retreat, and that no weaknesses would be tolerated. The battle turned out to be one of the most important of the war. In its first few days the British and French faced massive and sustained attacks by the Germans; after these attacks were contained, the tide of the battle started to turn.

The allies started to counterattack, and on September 9 the BEF and the French Fifth Army crossed the Marne. Over the next few days the Germans would be forced to retreat. The battle resulted in a victory for the Allies and finally halted the Germans in their tracks of their monthlong offensive. The six French armies and one British army succeeded in forcing the Germans to retreat from the Marne. Their bid for a quick victory over France was over.

The First Battle of the Marne was also significant in that airplanes were used for the first time in the war for reconnaissance missions. French pilots flew over the German lines and were able to report back on troop numbers, or areas of particular strength or weakness. Despite it being a victory for the Allies, the battle had exacted massive casualties, with an estimated 81,000 French soldiers killed and another 170,000 missing or wounded. The Germans had 220,000 casualties in total, and the British had 13,000 with 1,700 dead.

Engel's Seventy-Second Infantry Regiment had seen action in the First Battle of the Marne around the village of Maurupt-le-Montois, two hundred kilometers east of Paris. The Germans started their shelling there on September 6 and continued until September 10, totaling destroying the village. Engel's regiment suffered nearly eighteen hundred killed, wounded, missing, or captured. Unfortunately Engel was among the dead; he died on September 10 in Maurupt-le-Montois.

Engel wasn't the only famous cyclist who died that week. On the very same day that Engel was killed, Marceau Narcy—who had finished in twenty-second place in both the 1907 and 1908 Tours—died. He had enlisted with the Eighty-Second Infantry and fought at the Battle of the Marne. On September 12, just two days after the deaths of Engel and Narcy, another great cyclist, the Belgian Victor Fastre, was also killed in action. At the age of just nineteen, Fastre had won Liège–Bastogne–Liège in 1909 in controversial circumstances. Another Belgian, Eugène Charlier, had been first over the line, but was disqualified when race commissaires realized that he hadn't finished on the same bike that he started on. Victory was awarded to Fastre instead. He went on to race for the Alcyon team for a couple of seasons. Engel's brother Louis meanwhile would be one of the lucky ones to survive the war and take up racing again with some success. In 1920 he won Marseille–Lyon, and also a stage of San Sebastien–Madrid.

The exact details of how Engel died in the encounter are unknown, but on the day that he was killed later accounts reported that there had been hand-to-hand fighting between German and French troops in the village. A memorial was built in Maurupt-le-Montois three years after the end of the war to mark the sacrifice made by Engel and his comrades over those five days of fighting, which helped ensure that Paris wasn't captured. A plaque at the base reads, AT THIS PLACE, GERMAN MOMENTUM WAS BROKEN.

Scene from the Battle of the Somme.

"Going over the top," into a hail of enemy bullets.

5

The Foreign Legionnaire

The French Foreign Legion has always been arguably one of the most enigmatic divisions among all armed forces. Their reputation for toughness has been forged through their ruthless training regimes and also their exploits in various conflicts throughout the world. Traditionally recruiting officers were said to have asked few questions of new recruits regarding their backgrounds, and so the Legion developed a reputation as a safe haven for men trying to escape their troubles. The Legion was said to have attracted a lot of criminals including murderers, and also mercenary soldiers. As one writer would brutally put it, the Legion became "an ideal repository for the scum of the earth."

The *Légion étrangère* was formed in 1831, and became synonymous with various French colonial wars. The first image of many when they think of Legionnaires is of them in action in the Sahara Desert, wearing their distinctive *kepi blancs* to help ward off the heat of the sun. They did, however, fight with great distinction on French soil in both world wars.

Following the French entry into the war, the Legion opened up recruitment and was overwhelmed by applications. Thirty-two thousand foreigners signed up, among them almost a thousand Germans to willing to take up arms against their own countrymen. For a small country, Luxembourg also saw a considerable number join the fight. Luxembourg had declared its neutrality at the start of the war, but was still occupied by its enormous neighbor Germany. Many Luxembourgers felt that if Germany went on to win the war, their country would be annexed. This was the main reason why so many flocked to the Legion.

The winner of the 1909 Tour, François Faber, was among the estimated thirty-seven hundred from the Grand Duchy who signed up shortly after war had been declared. Faber had actually been born in France, in the small village of Aulnay-sur-Iton in Normandy. His mother, Marie-Paule, was from Lorraine, while his father, Jean-François, was from Luxembourg. He took his father's nationality but still considered himself French. François had an older half brother, Ernest Paul, who would also go on to become a professional cyclist.

The family would move to Colombes, northwest of Paris, while he was a child, and it was here that François started his cycling career in the amateur ranks, inspired in part by both his brother and the tales he had heard of the new Tour de France. While he raced as an

In 1909 François Faber became the first foreigner
to win the Tour de France .

amateur, François would work in numerous jobs to fund his exploits. He worked as a docker, waiter, shipbuilder, porter, and furniture mover, among other jobs. He soon made it to the professional ranks, signing for the Labor team prior to the 1906 season, at the age of just nineteen.

Shortly after he began to race, he was given the nickname "the Giant of Colombes." He stood nearly six feet tall and weighed two hundred pounds. The start of his career was fairly underwhelming: He didn't finish his first Tour de France, and had no results of note. However, in 1907, he finished in seventh place overall in the Tour. The following year was even better, as he won four stages of *La Grande Boucle* and finished in second place overall. He also had his first classic win later that season in the Tour of Lombardy. After an inauspicious start to his career, he had shown he had what it took to win the Tour.

He would go on to success in the Tour in 1909, in addition to finishing in second place twice. But the start of war stopped his cycling career in its tracks. He was still just twenty-eight years old when he joined the army and left his life in the peloton behind. Like many others, he thought that the situation with Germany would be resolved within a matter of months, and he would be able to get back to bike racing. Of course, this was not to be. In addition to winning the Tour de France, Faber claimed numerous classics victories, and he undoubtedly would have gone on to claim more had war not intervened.

Faber was assigned to the newly formed Deuxième Régiment de marche du Premier Régiment étranger, based at Avignon. This unit consisted of three volunteer battalions and one veteran battalion from Algeria. There were some difficulties integrating so many newcomers with battle-hardened veterans of Indochina and North Africa. The veterans regarded these newcomers with contempt, as they had never passed through the notorious training camp at Sidi Bel Abbès in northern Algeria. Still, Faber obviously impressed his superiors from early on, and he quickly moved up the ranks.

The regiment would see its first action at the Battle of the Marne in the commune of Sillery just a few weeks after its formation. Unlike so many others, Faber survived the battle, and soon afterward he received his promotion to corporal. His regiment would now settle in for what would become years of stalemate trench warfare. At the start of 1915 Faber was offered the post of cyclist for his company, but his reply was, "I prefer to serve in the trenches; I know all about trench work, and I have more chance of bringing down Germans there than as a cyclist."

After months of regular exposure to artillery fire from the Germans, the regiment's soldiers would eventually be relieved of their position in April 1915. However, they didn't have much time to recuperate: The following month they were sent into action again at the Battle of Artois.

Faber might have hoped to have spent some more time at home, as his wife was now heavily pregnant. Instead he was shipped back to the front to fight in what became known as the Second Battle of Artois. The battle would again see the French fight alongside the British; the two armies were jointly commanded by French generals Philippe Pétain and Joseph Joffre, along with General Douglas Haig of Great Britain.

The aim of the battle was twofold. Primarily the Allies wanted to dislodge the Germans from their commanding position on Vimy Ridge and gain access to the coalfields of Lens in the north. Second, at this stage in the war, the Russian army was struggling on the Eastern Front, and the Second Battle of Artois was also about trying to keep the Germans on the Western Front and ease the pressure on the Russians.

On his return to the front, Faber worked with his colleagues to help fortify the French trenches, build command posts, and lay telephone lines. He was popular among his fellow soldiers, who had heard of some of his legendary exploits from the Tour de France. His domination of the 1909 race was legendary.

Prior to that year's Tour, Lucien Petit-Breton had predicted that Faber would easily win the race. In the previous year's Tour—where he had finished second overall behind Petit-Breton—Faber had taken four stages, and he seemed to be getting better and better. They had both been members of the dominant Peugeot team, but at the end of the season Faber signed for Alcyon. Late in the season Faber went on to take victory in the Tour of Lombardy.

The 1909 Tour started off with a stage from Paris to Roubaix, and on a day of torrential rain victory went to Cyrille Van Houwaert, who became the first Belgian to win a stage of the race. The terrible weather continued over the next number of days, and it played into Faber's hands. He took victory on the second stage to Metz; his winning streak continued for the next four stages all the way to Nice. The win at Metz had been impressive: He led the race alone for 200 of the 398 kilometers.

It was a reflection of the terrible conditions the riders had to endure that seventy-seven of them abandoned during the first six stages. The third started in temperatures hovering just above freezing, and on that stage over the Ballon d'Alsace in the Vosges, Faber finished more than thirty-three minutes ahead of the next racer. He described crossing the Ballon d'Alsace afterward: "It disappeared into the murk and, as I reached it, snow was blanketing the summit."

The next stage took the riders from Belfort to Lyon, and it was another epic performance from the Luxembourger. Three thousand spectators turned up at 2 AM to see the riders off. Faber crossed the Col de Porte alone, despite being blown off his bike twice and also kicked off by a horse. He was unhurt, though, and continued on. He struggled through torrential rain and would also break his chain that day, but despite all of this the others were unable to catch him.

A reported twenty thousand fans were at the finish in Lyon to witness his victory.

He struggled somewhat with the heat of southern France for the next couple of stages, and had injuries from another crash to contend with as well. However, he again won a stage from Bayonne to Bordeaux to consolidate his lead. While Faber struggled on the middle stages of the race, his half brother Ernest Paul stepped up to the mark and won the stage to Nîmes. Paul would go on to finish the race in sixth place overall.

Faber's new Alcyon team had also emerged as the new dominant force in cycling, winning an incredible thirteen out of a total fourteen stages that year. Faber rode into Paris on the last stage with a comfortable lead over second-place Gustave Garrigou to take victory. This was despite a final mishap: Faber broke his chain with a kilometer to go. He had to run the final stretch with his bike to the finish line in the Parc des Princes, where he was mobbed by adoring fans.

His gutsy win had been lauded by all who witnessed it, but French journalist Gérard Ejnès would allude to the fact that the win may not have been as clean as it seemed. He would say years afterward, "Nobody would go as far as saying he achieved such an exploit on just water, but in those days everything was permitted." It wasn't a secret that the use of drugs by cyclists was quite common.

Faber's biggest supporter on the race had been his mother, Marie-Paule, who was seen embracing him at the end of a number of the stage finishes. "The good mother Faber," as she became known, started to become a feature in the reports of each day's racing in *L'Auto*. Marie-Paule had turned up at the stage finish in Metz to witness her son's victory "against his express wishes," and she also turned up at the end of the race in Paris, where François and his older brother were reported as "devouring her with caresses. It brought tears to the happy mother's eyes."

François Faber (centre) alongside other sports stars who would join the fight. Jean Bouin, who won an Olympic 1500m medal is on the left and World Champion boxer Georges Carpentier is on the right.

In *L'Auto* they wrote: "François Faber's Tour de France victory will long remain in the memory. His feats will find no imitators in the near future. Let us praise the Giant from Colombes because he was from start to finish the master of every situation. Let us praise him because, throughout the entire 4,488 kilometers of the Tour, he remained invincible and unflinching. Let us praise this 22-year old as a great man who deserves the triumphant greeting that met him everywhere."

It seemed that the victory had taken a lot out of Faber, as he badly needed a long rest. He told one race official, Alphonse Steinès, of his plans after the race: "I know an excellent little place to go fishing in the Sens area and that's where I'm going to be from tomorrow onwards. You won't see me again before September, for the classics of the end of the season."

After his victory that year Faber had apparently received hundreds of letters, poems, and even some marriage proposals from admirers. A biography of him was released titled *Le géant de la route*. His name, as with the other Tour winners who preceded him, became known throughout France, and in Luxembourg he was asked by the government to lecture on the benefits of cycling. In the following year he would go on to take victory in the big classics Paris–Roubaix, Bordeaux–Paris, and Paris–Tours.

In the 1910 Tour, Faber would challenge for victory, but his chances were scuppered by a collision with a dog. He won three stages that year and led the race for eleven stages, but the crash at Nîmes ruined his hopes. Faber meanwhile had to cope with his injuries for the next eight stages, and eventually lost the lead to Octave Lapize on the twelfth stage to Nantes. The next year he would win two stages of the Tour, but his days as a genuine overall contender were over.

Faber regaled his fellow soldiers with stories from his epic victories, and it would help ease the tension of battle. However, even Faber could do little to quell the fearful apprehension that they felt prior to the battle in Artois. On May 9, after the largest artillery bombardment of the war to date, four battalions of the Foreign Legion—seventy-five officers and 3,822 enlisted men, Faber among them—launched an assault on the German lines. Nineteen fifteen was the first year of large-scale trench warfare, and these assaults—essentially suicide missions—would help to contribute to losses of 350,000 French soldiers in that year alone.

That morning Faber waited anxiously with his colleagues for the French artillery to cease firing, which would give them the signal that they would be going over the top. He had witnessed enough carnage at the Battle of the Marne to understand that there was a good chance he might not make it. Within twenty-four hours of the start of their engagement, only eighteen hundred of the original four thousand men were still in a position to fight.

As with the 1910 Tour de France, and the introduction of stages through the Pyrénées, Faber's six-foot frame would once more prove a significant disadvantage. His height made him an easier target for the enemy infantrymen.

Another Legionnaire who was also a member of the Premier Regiment, Kiffin Rockwell, later described the initial part of the battle. Rockwell was an American who along with his brother, Paul, had offered his services to France by letter to the French consul-general in New Orleans. He was injured on the first day of fighting at Artois, and would have to spend six weeks in hospital. In a letter Rockwell sent home, he wrote:

> *In a few minutes it began to sound as if all hell had broken loose, when our artillery all along the line opened up on the Germans. The damnedest bombardment imaginable was kept up until ten o'clock. Along the whole German line, you could see nothing but smoke and debris. At ten o'clock, I saw the finest sight I have ever seen. It was the men from the* Premier Étranger *crawling out of our trenches, with their bayonets glittering against the sun, and advancing on the Bosches. There was not a sign of hesitation. They were falling fast, but as fast as men fell, it seemed as if new men sprang up out of the ground to take their places. One second it looked as if an entire section had fallen by one sweep of a machine gun. In a few moments a second line of men*

crawled out of our trenches; and at seven minutes
past ten, our captain called "En avant!" [Forward!]
and we went dashing down the trenches with the
German artillery giving us hell as we went.

It's difficult for us to comprehend what Faber and his colleagues must have been thinking as they waited to go over the top, knowing that they faced near-certain death. It had rained heavily in the days preceding the start of the battle, making progress toward the Germans even tougher.

A number of different stories would circulate afterward as to how Faber had met his end. One was that he had received a telegram from his wife announcing the birth of his daughter and, overjoyed at the news, jumped up from the trench—only to be shot by a German sniper. This story is untrue, however; he had learned of his daughter's birth four days earlier.

Another story was that he was carrying an injured colleague back from no-man's-land when he was shot. One of Faber's comrades was shot between Carency and Mont-Sant-Éloi, and upon hearing his screams for help, Faber made his way over to the injured man. He lifted him to his shoulders and had almost made it back to his trench when he was felled by a German bullet. This account contradicts a newspaper account from the time, however, which mentions that he was involved in an attack on the White House defenses in Carency: "According to a letter from the front, Faber was in the first line which led the attack on the White House fortifications on Sunday, May 9, when he fell by the side of his officer. After the battle, in which the German losses were 25,000, including 1,300 prisoners, Faber did not respond to the roll-call. His body has not been found, but there appears to be no doubt that he has been killed."

Faber's battalion received the order at 10 AM, and after some tough fighting, they reached their objective. Once the smoke cleared, a friend of Faber's by the name of Georges Miron—a motorcycle rider—witnessed a battlefield strewn with corpses and wounded soldiers. Miron made his way to a first-aid station at nearby Bertonval to look for his friend. A soldier called Noire told him that Faber had been beside him at one stage during the battle, and had cried out, "I've been hit." He fell holding his hands to his stomach; that was the last that Noire had seen of him.

Miron personally told another cyclist, Louis Darragon, who was stationed in the same sector, the news that Faber was missing, presumably dead. Faber was friends with Darragon and had raced against him on numerous occasions. Darragon had also achieved some great results, including two wins in the Motor Paced World Championships. He would die just three years later in a crash at the Vélodrome d'Hiver in Paris.

Another cyclist based in the sector, Charles Cruchon, had finished in the top ten of the Tour twice, as well as winning the Tour of Belgium. Cruchon helped Miron try to find Faber's body, but to no avail. Cruchon had also taken part in the 1914 Tour, where he finished in thirty-fifth place. Faber was the first Tour winner to be killed during the war. He must have had a bad feeling about the attack as the night before, he had given his personal documents to Georges Miron.

The French had suffered massive casualties in the battle for no gains. Between May 9 and June 16, 1915, they estimated their losses at the battle to be nearly 17,000 soldiers and officers killed, 20,500 missing (which usually meant killed), and another 63,500 wounded. Faber's regiment would suffer major casualties: 1,950 soldiers out of a total of 2,900 would be killed.

Faber's body was never found, but it is possible that he is interred alongside the twenty thousand other unidentified casualties at the cemetery at Notre Dame de Lorette. There is a small plaque in his memory in the church at the cemetery, which overlooks Vimy Ridge. Faber would be posthumously awarded the Médaille Militaire. He is also remembered by the race named after him, the Grand Prix François Faber, which takes place in Luxembourg.

Although he had won the Tour de France for Luxembourg, he died for his adopted country, France. The 1909 Tour winner would never get to see his newborn child. To this day the man who dominated that year's Tour still holds the record for the most consecutive stage wins in the race.

A French general inspects a trench.

It could be difficult to identify the dead after battles,
and the bodies of many cyclists would never be found.

6

Survivor

In 2004 the Tour de France started in Liège with a prologue; the opening road stages would also take place in Belgium. Prior to the *Grand Départ*, a Belgian newspaper interviewed the oldest living Tour de France participant. As it turned out and unbeknownst to the journalist, apart from being the oldest Tour cyclist Émile Brichard also happened to be one of the oldest First World War veterans. Unlike many of the other Tour de France veterans who fought in the First World War, Brichard's time as a professional cyclist didn't come until years later.

Brichard was born in the village of Arsimont, halfway between Charleroi and Namur, in 1899. In August 1914, like many other towns and villages, Arsimont would witness numerous atrocities by the invading German army. One hundred twenty-six houses were demolished, and thirteen locals were killed. Brichard's father decided that the family would have to escape, and they were fortunate enough to be able to sail across the North Sea to England. They settled in Wolverhampton in the Midlands, and young Émile was able to find employment in a factory manufacturing boots for the British army.

The year after his homeland had been invaded, Brichard signed up to fight with the British army. He was assigned to the Fourth Battalion of the Royal Army Medical Corps in July 1915, and soon found himself back in Belgium, at the coastal town of De Panne. There he worked at the military hospital L'Océan, which had been founded by Dr. Antoine Depage and Queen Elizabeth of Belgium. Brichard would meet the queen while he worked there.

The hospital relied upon ongoing funding from the Red Cross, but it also needed soldiers such as Brichard to help. British soldiers helped with driving and heavy duties such as moving wounded soldiers. The same year that Brichard had started working at the hospital, Marie Depage—the wife of the founder—traveled to the United States to raise funds for the Red Cross. She toured a number of big cities and was able to raise the incredible amount of one hundred thousand dollars. For her return journey from New York to Europe, she could choose between two ships: the *Lapland* and the *Lusitania*. She chose the latter. On May 7, as she was nearing the end of her crossing, the *Lusitania* was torpedoed by a U-boat off the coast of Ireland with the loss of 1,195 lives, including Marie.

Although he didn't serve at the front, Brichard witnessed the horrors of war via the thousands of badly injured soldiers who passed through L'Océan. He left the army a year after the war's end and, instead of returning to England, stayed on in his native Belgium. He initially found work as a miner, but in his spare time he started cycling. He would later recount his first few years in the sport: "I rarely raced outside the Sambre-Meuse region, and despite the fact that I never won races, I became a professional."

At the time, Brichard was friends with Adelin Benoit, who had won a stage of the 1925 Tour, and in 1926, he won Bordeaux–Paris. Benoit persuaded his Alcyon-Peugeot team to also sign his friend, where he would race alongside some of the greats of the time, including the winner of the 1927 and 1928 Tours, Nicolas Frantz. To his surprise, Brichard was selected for that year's Tour de France. For the first time ever, the Tour would start outside Paris, in Évian-les-Bains, but before they departed by train to the start town they would parade down the Champs-Élysées. Despite the race having taken place seventy-eight years earlier, Brichard could still recall the train journey to the start in the Alps in his 2004 interview: "I remember that the area was nice and that there was a lake."

It would be the longest Tour ever, at 5,745 kilometers, and it started with a 373-kilometer stage from Évian-les-Bains to Mulhouse. Italian star Ottavio Bottechia took off on his own early on in the stage, but would falter later. He wasn't the only one struggling. Brichard had never seen climbs like those in the Jura Mountains before. "The Col de la Faucille was very difficult, and the spectators were helping us by pushing us."

He punctured twice on the climb, and ended up having to rip the tire from the rim, fix the puncture, and sew the tire back up. He lost a lot of time, but persevered. However, he suffered more punctures and ran out of spare tires. He struggled on with a flat tire but, losing more and more time, eventually was forced to retire.

He said, "I was hoping to at least stay in the race until the north of France, near to my home. I returned home and didn't tell anybody about my performance because I was embarrassed. I never participated in any other big race."

He wasn't the only rider to abandon on the first stage. Another notable cyclist to pull out of the race that day was Kisso Kawamuro, the first Japanese rider to enter the Tour. (It wouldn't be until 2009 that the first Japanese riders would finish the race.) The race was won by fellow Belgian Lucien Buysse, who had first entered back in 1914.

Brichard retired from cycling shortly after his Tour appearance and opened up a liquor shop a few years later with his wife. They would separate a few years later, and he lost many of his mementos from the war and his cycling career. He would continue to follow cycling on TV and considered Eddy Merckx among his favorite riders. He would later remarry, though, and despite telling his second wife when he was a hundred years old that he wanted a divorce, they would stay together until she died two years before him. When asked the secret of his longevity, he replied, "I like a good drink, and I like women."

As the years passed, and fewer and fewer Belgian veterans turned up at the country's commemoration of the Armistice every year, Brichard still never mentioned that he had taken part. Only during the conversation with the Belgian journalist in 2004 did he speak of his role in the war. That was when the realization came that Brichard must be one of the few veterans still alive. It turned out that there was only one other living Belgian First World War veteran: Cyrillus-Camillus Barbary, who had served on the Western Front, emigrated to the United States after the war, and died just two months after Brichard.

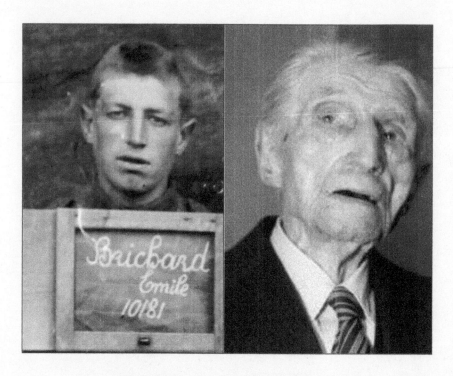

Emile Brichard, in youth and old age:
one of the last-surviving Belgian veterans of the war.

When Brichard's story emerged, numerous journalists and TV crews visited him at his home in Gerpinnes, just south of Charleroi, to hear his story. It was a lot to deal with for a 104-year-old man, and two days after the Tour de France left Belgian soil, he passed away. He had stayed alive just long enough to ensure that his story would not be forgotten.

7

The Aussies

The onset of war meant that the two Australians who had taken part in the 1914 Tour de France, Iddo "Snowy" Munro and Donald Kirkham, would not get another chance to do so. Upon the outbreak of hostilities, they both returned to their homeland. They had left Australia back in December of the previous year along with four other riders, Charlie Piercey, George Bell, Charles Snell, and Fred Keefe. The other four hadn't made it to the start line of the Tour but they did get their share of big race experience. Prior to the Tour de France, they had taken part in Milan–San Remo, Paris–Roubaix, and Paris–Brussels, among other races. It had been very different from what they were used to in Australia.

Munro and Kirkham, in particular, had pleased their sponsors with their performances throughout the season. At the end of the Tour, the Gladiator Company had written an open letter expressing their satisfaction with the performance of the pair. Kirkham had finished in seventeenth position, with Munro three places farther back, and Gladiator offered the pair of them a contract to take part in the 1915 Tour.

Keefe would describe their experience afterward:

> When we got to France, we discovered for one thing, that the distance of their shortest important open race was within a mile of our longest—Warnambool to Melbourne. Then again, the roads of France and Belgium proved a great disappointment to us. We all expected to find smooth, hard, dustless highways, whose surface would compare with the first-class racing tracks of Australia. Instead, we found that the best Australian courses were quite the equal of the leading French metaled stretches, while there seemed to be endless miles of what is known as pavé, which is surely an invention of the evil one himself. This pavé consists simply of small blocks of stone set in the road without any remarkable degree of evenness, on which the vibration caused by riding and speed is beyond imagination. How we Australians sighed for once-despised roads of our homeland after our experience.

Iddo 'Snowy' Munro, along with Donald Kirkham,
were the first Australians to finish the Tour.

docks, and a reception was held for them that night. The celebrations finished with a toast to the king and the singing of the national anthem. It was the last night that many of the club mates would spend in one another's company, as a considerable number had signed up to fight.

Not long after the cyclists returned to Australia, the first troops of the Australian Imperial Force (AIF) would be setting sail in the opposite direction. Days after Britain entered the war, the Australian army had started recruitment. By August 20, 1914, more than ten thousand men had enlisted, but all had to undergo a medical before being accepted. Among the requirements were that they had to be of a certain height, have good teeth, and not have flat feet.

Upon his return Munro would also try to sign up to fight for Australia alongside the Allies, and like so many other cyclists he wanted to become a pilot. The Australian Flying Corps (AFC) had been established in 1912, and later that year a Central Flying School was established in Point Cook, Victoria, where pilot training took place. During the war Australian pilots were busy on a number of fronts. They began operations in Mesopotamia, and would also see action in Egypt, Palestine, and the Western Front.

Fortunately, or unfortunately, depending on how you look at it, Munro failed the medical. The doctors found that he had flat feet and turned him down—even though he was volunteering as a pilot, not an infantryman (who might have been required to march long distances). He tried again a short while later, but the doctors came to the same conclusion. Despite his extreme fitness, there would be no war for Munro.

It's not known whether Kirkham also tried to enlist. During those opening months of the war, the army was so inundated with volunteers that recruitment officers were forced to turn people away. As the war went on, however, and news emerged of the slaughter of thousands of young men, recruitment dried up. By 1916 the AIF was short of men, and a referendum was held to determine whether conscription should be introduced. The proposal was narrowly beaten, as was a second referendum the following year.

The World War One campaign with which Australian forces would become most synonymous was the disastrous Battle of Gallipoli in 1915. The British and French wanted to secure a sea route to Russia via the Black Sea. This would require passage through the Dardanelles—the narrow passage linking the Mediterranean to the Black Sea. First Lord of the Admiralty Winston Churchill proposed a naval attack here that would prove to be disastrous. The Allies severely underestimated the strength of the Turkish forces and the resistance they would put up, and ended up roundly beaten.

Neither Munro nor Kirkham was involved in the Gallipoli campaign, but a number of Tour de France cyclists did fight there. Prior to the start of hostilities, French troops had joined Australian and British forces (which included many Indian, Canadian, and Irish divisions) in Egypt, while their generals devised plans for landing on the peninsula. On April 25, 1915, the Australian Imperial Force, along with troops from Britain, France, and New Zealand, landed at Gallipoli. On the same day, the French forces landed at Kum Kale on the Asian side of the straits. Despite some initial progress by the Allies, they would be beaten back and forced to withdraw in December of the same year.

In addition to the 35,000 British and 11,500 ANZAC (Australian and New Zealand Army Corps) troops killed, nearly 10,000 French soldiers died at Gallipoli along with 17,000 wounded. Among those who had been fighting in the Dardanelles was René Etien, who had taken part in the 1912 Tour as an independent. He didn't get too far in that edition, though: He finished in eighty-ninth position on the opening stage from Paris to Dunkirk, one hour and eighteen minutes behind the winner Charles Crupelandt. The next day he would finish in 106th place, and on the third stage he withdrew on the road to Belfort. He never returned to the race. Etien had signed up for the Fifty-Sixth Colonial Infantry, and he died not long after the start of the invasion, on May 6, 1915, during the Second Battle of Krithia.

Another French cyclist who died from injuries sustained in the Gallipoli invasion was Maurice Dejoie. He had been a member of the Clement-Dunlop team in the 1914 Tour but retired on the third stage. He died in November 1915 on the Greek island of Lemnos, fifty kilometers from Gallipoli, which had been used by the British and French as a base. The exact details of his death are unknown.

While the Australian army is forever linked with Gallipoli, its involvement in action on the Western Front can sometimes be overlooked. A famous cyclist who did end up fighting for the Australians in France and Belgium was Englishman Tom Gascoyne. He had started bike racing back in 1893 and would go on to set a number of world records, including that for twenty-five miles, which he covered in fifty-seven minutes and eighteen seconds in 1896. A few years later he raced in America, where he managed to beat the famous Major Taylor twice. Gascoyne was originally from Chesterfield in Derbyshire, but in his twenties he moved to Australia with his young family in search of a better life. He originally lived in New South Wales before moving to Preston, a suburb of Melbourne.

In February 1916, at the age of thirty-nine, Gascoyne signed up to fight for his adopted country. When he enlisted, Gascoyne indicated that the majority of his pay should be paid directly to his wife, Linda, and their young family. He was assigned to the Twenty-First Battalion, which had been formed the year before. After an intense period of training at Broadmeadows, Victoria, they were shipped to Europe. Gascoyne had missed out on the fighting at Gallipoli, where the Twenty-First had landed at ANZAC Cove. The battle had finished just a month before he signed up.

By the time Gascoyne joined, the battalion had moved on to France, where they would be the first Australians to commence operations on the Western Front. Their first action was at the Battle of Pozières, northeast of Amiens. In just seven weeks of fighting, the Australians would suffer twenty-three thousand casualties, including sixty-eight hundred dead. It was a similar number to the total deaths at Gallipoli over eight months. Australian historian Charles Bean would say that the Pozières ridge "is more densely sown with Australian sacrifice than any other place on earth." Gascoyne was one of the fortunate ones to survive the battle.

The following year would see the Twenty-First in action at Bullecourt, south of Arras; later in the year they would redeploy to Belgium, to the Ypres Salient. On October 4, 1917, a German counteroffensive began near Ypres. The intention of Operation Hohensturm was to capture the area around the village of Zonnebeke. Gascoyne, who had been a corporal in the Twenty-First Battalion, was among those who sought to defend the area. The exact details of what happened during the battle are unclear, but unfortunately Gascoyne was killed in the action on the day that the operation commenced. His body was not found.

Ten years after the battle, in 1927, the Menin Gate was built in Ypres as a memorial to the missing British and Commonwealth soldiers from the Ypres Salient. A total of 54,896 men had their names engraved on the monument. Such were the numbers of men missing in action around Ypres, it was found that as vast as the Menin Gate was, it wasn't nearly big enough to hold the names of all missing soldiers. A cutoff point of August 15, 1917, was chosen; the names of soldiers missing after this date are engraved on the Tyne Cot memorial instead.

Although he died in October of that year, the name of Tom Gascoyne appears on the Menin Gate memorial in Panel 93. It may not be there forever, however. Every year around Ypres, bodies of missing soldiers are found, often during construction work. The authorities try to determine who the person is through the use of DNA; if they succeed, a military funeral is held, and the man's name is removed from the Menin Gate. There is always a slim chance that Gascoyne's body might be found someday, and that he can be given a proper burial.

After the war, meanwhile, Kirkham went on to train with Hubert Opperman, who would be among the next generation of Australian cyclists to take part in the Tour de France, in 1928. Unfortunately Kirkham was hit by a drunk driver while out cycling in 1924, and he subsequently developed pneumonia and tuberculosis prior to his death five years later. Munro meanwhile established a taxi company in Melbourne, which still exists to this day. He would also to work to promote cycling in Australia until his death in 1980.

8

The Fighter Pilot

The first decade of the Tour de France coincided with the pioneering days of an invention that had an enormous impact on society. The Wright brothers took the first-ever powered human flight just a few months after the inaugural Tour. In the years that followed, rapid advancements would be made in the field of aviation.

Seven years later at the Tour de France, the French cyclist Octave Lapize would get his first taste of flight. It was during the 1910 Tour, which he would go on to win, that Lapize experienced flying an airplane. On a rest day prior to the final stage of 262 kilometers from Caen to Paris, an aviation festival was taking place, and the race leader was offered the opportunity to join famous aviator Léon Morane for a short flight. Lapize was leading the race overall, and some felt that by partaking in such activities he was rubbing the other cyclists' noses in it. However, it seemed he had a genuine interest in flight. Morane was one of the pioneers of flight in France and would set a world altitude record shortly after his encounter with Lapize. A photo of the two appeared in *La Vie au Grand Air* shortly afterward. Morane's airplane was manufactured by the company set up by Louis Blériot— the man who just a year previously had become a hero in France when he successfully crossed the English Channel for the first time.

Louis Octave Lapize was born in Montrouge in the fourteenth arrondissement of Paris on October 24, 1887. His father, also Octave, worked long hours in a nearby brewery and expected the same strong work ethic from his son after he left school at age fourteen. He worked alongside his father at the brewery for a time, and enjoyed the physical labor. However, Lapize—who'd been given the nick-named "Le Frise'l" for his curly hair—could become easily distracted by his newfound love of the sport of cycling.

His father had no patience with such trivial pastimes, and Octave had to train in secret. He even signed up with the French Amateur Cyclists' Federation, unbeknownst to his father. Lapize senior eventually found out, and it resulted in many arguments between father and son. He was undeterred, though, and continued to train hard. His father's opinion would change when he took a big victory in a race in Villiers in 1906.

It was 1907 when Lapize really came to prominence: That year he won both the national amateur road and cyclo-cross titles. It was enough to gain selection for the following year's Olympics in London, where he took home the bronze medal in the 100-kilometer track race. That year he also won a prestigious track race for amateurs, the Bol d'Or. He turned professional afterward for the Biguet-Dunlop team.

Lapize was successful as a professional from the start, winning Paris–Roubaix, Paris–Dreux, and Milan–Varese in his debut year, 1909, as well as finishing fourth in the Tour of Lombardy. He also took part in his first Tour de France that year. On the opening stage to Roubaix, he came in third and went one better on the following stage to Metz, finishing in second place, thirty-three minutes behind François Faber. However, he pulled out of the race in appalling weather on just the third stage.

Lapize continued to also be successful on the track, as he won numerous six-day races including those of Paris and Brussels, set a number of motor-paced world records, and continued to win cyclo-cross races. His manager, Paul Ruinart, said of him, "Lapize will be the best rider of his generation. He can and must win everything because he has all the gifts of a perfect cyclist."

Lapize had a successful start to his second season in 1910 as he again took victory in Paris–Roubaix and finished second in Paris–Brussels. Despite it being just his second season as a professional, he would go into that year's Tour as one of the favorites. By this time he had signed for the incredibly strong Alcyon-Dunlop team that also included the race's previous two winners, François Faber and Lucien Petit-Breton, in addition to other great cyclists such as Eugène

The 1910 Tour winner Octave Lapize, would become famous
for yelling "Vous êtes des assassins! Oui, des assassins!'
at Tour officials at the top of the Col du Tourmalet.

Christophe, Paul Duboc, and Gustave Garrigou.

That year's Tour was the first time that the race would venture into the high mountains. A number of months prior to the start, Desgrange had dispatched his assistant at *L'Auto*, Alphonse Steinès, on a reconnaissance trip to the Pyrénées. Steinès had been involved in drawing up the course since its inception in 1903, and it had been his suggestion to include some of the Pyrenean climbs in the race. Desgrange had initially considered the idea sheer lunacy, but eventually warmed to it.

Steinès arrived at an inn near to the Col du Tourmalet at the end of January, and asked the owner for directions. The innkeeper told him that it was difficult enough to cross in July, let alone in winter. Steinès decided to persevere and hired a car to travel over the pass. As the sun was setting, however, he had to come to a halt near to the top due to heavy snow. He pressed on nonetheless by foot in snow four meters deep, and at one stage fell into a ravine. Steinès was now in trouble. "I was lost and alone in the darkness. I didn't want to die on a hostile, unknown mountain at an altitude of 2,255 meters."

Luckily for Steinès, however, search parties were sent up the mountain to look for him; he was found disheveled at 3 AM. He was helped down the mountain, where the locals gave him food and helped to warm him up. Despite his remarkable adventure and near-death experience the night before, the following morning Steinès sent the famous telegram to Desgrange in Paris that read: "Crossed Tourmalet. Very Good Road. Perfectly Passable. Signed Steines." This was the green light for the race to enter the high mountains for the first time.

It's difficult to understand why Steinès would have sent that message to Desgrange given his experiences of the night before, but perhaps it was the fear of telling his paymaster that his idea of routing the race through the mountains was unworkable and his journey had been a waste of time and money. Regardless, the entry into the mountains that year would make the Tour even more epic than it was already. Shortly afterward, Desgrange announced in *L'Auto* that the race would traverse the climbs of the Col d'Aspin, the Col de Peyresourde, the Col d'Aubisque, and the Col du Tourmalet. Both organizers and government authorities provided funds for the Pyrenean roads to be paved in the month leading up to the race to make them a little more roadworthy than they had been for Steinès.

The eighth edition of the race traveled clockwise around the country, comprised fifteen stages, and took place over four weeks. The winner was widely expected to come from the ranks of Lapize's formidable Alcyon team—most likely Lapize's new teammate, the 1909 winner, François Faber.

One hundred and ten riders had started the race in Paris on July 3, and once again the race would be decided on points. Initially there had been 136 entrants, but 26 of these withdrew when they heard the news of the race venturing into the Pyrénées. Journalists had been writing about these stages using terms such as *dangerous* and *bizarre*, increasing the levels of anxiety. There were three teams with ten riders each; the rest of the peloton was made up of independents or *isolés*. The race became an epic duel between Lapize and Faber.

The race started off well for Lapize, who finished third on the first stage to Roubaix. This was despite his collision with a cow that had wandered onto the road. (Lapize escaped relatively unscathed.) He repeated his third-place finish on the next stage of 398 kilometers to Metz to move into second place on General Classification behind Faber.

However, on the third stage to Belfort, which crossed over the Ballon d'Alsace, he could only manage sixth place, while Faber finished in second. While he maintained his third place overall, he slipped farther behind his teammate, reigning champion Faber. It looked like it might be all over for him after the fourth stage to Lyon—he slipped farther down the field as Faber took the stage win to consolidate his lead—but Lapize's form started to show on the fifth stage, from Lyon to Grenoble. Lapize was suffering terribly with sore feet but nevertheless managed to stay with the lead group while Faber was dropped. Desgrange was to say of the lead group that "they rode brilliantly, like men possessed." Lapize's strength that day took its toll on the others, and one by one they too dropped.

Lapize punctured near the end, but continued on with a flat tire to win his first Tour stage. He was five hours ahead of the last man to finish. His feet were now in such a bad way that he had to hobble to his nearby hotel. He was back in third place overall, and Faber had a real battle on his hands. Fans throughout the country were captivated by the contest; circulation for *L'Auto* increased even more.

Unfortunately tragedy struck the Tour de France that year. On the rest day after the stage to Nice, one of the cyclists, Adolphe Hélière, went for a swim in the Mediterranean and died. Some say he was stung by a jellyfish, while others claim he either drowned or had a stroke. In any event, he became the first person to die on the race.

While Lapize's form improved, Faber was struck by bad luck. On the 345-kilometer seventh stage from Nice to Nîmes he hit a dog and crashed. He continued and won the stage, while Lapize finished in third. However, Faber's injuries were worse than he'd originally thought and would affect him for the remainder of the race.

One welcome addition to that year's race was the introduction by Desgrange of the *voiture-balai,* the broom wagon. Riders who abandoned—and plenty did—could use this following vehicle to take them and their bike to the finish line.

The ninth stage of the race from Perpignan to Luchon saw the riders tackling the Col de Port, the Portet d'Aspet, and the Portet des Ares. Lapize's ability as a climber came to the fore. He finished eighteen minutes ahead of Émile Georget and a further four minutes ahead of Faber. Yet for all his efforts and despite the big time gap, he gained only a couple of points on the Luxembourger.

It was the epic tenth stage from Luchon to Bayonne that was to become one of the most legendary stages ever and where Lapize was to utter his immortal words. The stage was 326 kilometers long and took in the climbs of the Peyresourde, Aspin, Tourmalet, and Aubisque. Desgrange departed for Paris prior to the stage, possibly out of fear of the riders' reactions to the course, and instead asked his employees to supervise.

The riders departed at 3:30 AM. Lapize was the first to attack and the first rider to cross both the Col de Peyresourde and the Col d'Aspin. However, he was caught after the Aspin by his teammate Gustave Garrigou; the two ascended the Tourmalet mano a mano. Lapize eventually dropped his breakaway companion to cross alone. About a hundred spectators had made their way to the top of the climb to witness Lapize become the first man to crest the summit in the Tour, albeit walking with his bike. Even though he was behind Lapize on the road, Gustave Garrigou managed to reach the top of the climb without dismounting; for his efforts he received a prize of one hundred francs.

On the final climb of the day, the Col d'Aubisque, Lapize was caught and passed by a local rider, François Lafourcade, from nearby Lahontan, who became the first rider to cross the mountain. Fifteen minutes later Lapize approached and uttered what would become one of the most famous quotes in the sport. Another of Desgrange's assistants, Victor Breyer, described the scene at the top of the climb as they waited for the next man after Lafourcade to arrive.

Still the minutes passed. Another quarter-hour passed before the second rider appeared, whom we immediately recognized as Lapize. Unlike Lafourcade, Lapize was walking, half leaning on, half pushing his machine. His eyes revealed an intense distress. But unlike his predecessor, Lapize spoke, and in abundance. "You are assassins, yes, assassins." To discuss matters with a man in this condition would have been cruel and stupid. I walked at his side, attentive to all he said. After more imprecations, he finished by saying, "Don't worry, at Eaux-Bonnes [the town at the bottom of the mountain] I'm going to quit."

Some accounts say, that Lapize also said to Breyer, "Tell Desgrange from me, you cannot ask human beings to do a thing like this."

However, Lapize must have thought better of his threat on the descent: He didn't quit. The finish was still 175 kilometers away, though—easily far enough for him to catch Lafourcade, which he duly did. He won the stage ahead of Pierino Albini with Faber in third. Lapize was now in second place overall, but still ten points behind Faber.

Two days later the riders faced a 269-kilometer stage from Bayonne to Bordeaux, and Lapize made more inroads on Faber's lead as he finished in seventh place while Faber came home three places down. After eleven stages, Faber's lead was down to just seven points—and that was reduced further to just one point after the stage to Nantes. Faber was now struggling with his injuries from the dog collision. The Giant of Colombes was looking vulnerable. Their battle had really captured the imagination of the French public by now, and daily sales of *L'Auto* were reaching two hundred thousand.

Having held the lead for three weeks, Faber would finally be overtaken by Lapize on the thirteenth stage, to Brest. Lapize finished in fifth place, a clear ten minutes ahead of his rival. There were now three points between them. Both men tried to recover in Brest before the final two days, but to all race followers Lapize seemed to be in the ascendancy and surely in line for the victory.

On the penultimate stage, to Caen, Faber attacked early and built up a lead of twenty minutes. It looked like he might retake the lead, until bad luck struck again and he punctured twice. He was caught by Lapize and some others and would eventually crack. Lapize took his fourth stage win of the race while Faber finished in fourth, six points behind Lapize.

Lapize now held a comfortable lead ahead of the final stage to Paris. Not long after the start in Caen, however, he punctured, and Faber decided to take advantage of his teammate's misfortune. He attacked along with seven others; if he was to win the stage and Lapize didn't catch anybody ahead of him, then victory would go to Faber. By the halfway point at Rouen, things were looking bad for Lapize: The gap between him and the leaders, including Faber, was now twelve minutes.

The race started to turn in his favor, though, as riders started to get dropped and he overtook them one by one. In the end, Faber could only manage fourth on the stage, while Lapize clawed his way back to finish just two places behind and take the overall win. It had been an epic race and the closest finish in the Tour to date.

For his efforts, Lapize won 5,000 francs for the overall victory and earned a total of 7,525 francs throughout the race. He also received considerable bonus money from Alcyon and Dunlop. His earnings from the race were a quite remarkable sum at a time when average daily wages in France were around five to seven francs. His opinion of Desgrange from earlier in the race hadn't changed by the time they reached Paris, however; as he told one journalist, "Desgrange is truly a murderer."

Remarkably enough, it was the one and only time that Lapize would manage to finish the Tour. He took part every year from 1909 to 1914 but abandoned each time, except for the year that he won. He did go on to take two more stage wins, though: the sixth stage to Nice in 1912 and the eighth stage to Marseille in 1914. One of the reasons he struggled was that he thought other riders ganged up on him; as he was to say, "When I stop for a piss, they all take to their heels. When someone else stops, they take no notice."

Despite not taking overall victory in the Tour again, Lapize enjoyed other notable successes in addition to his Tour stage wins. He won Paris–Roubaix for the third year in succession in 1911. He also took a hat trick of victories in Paris–Brussels, winning in 1911, 1912, and 1913. He was still only twenty-seven years old when the war started and could have looked forward to more significant wins.

Within two weeks of the start of hostilities, Lapize had signed up to fight, and was assigned to the Nineteenth Squadron of the Army Service Corps, automobile division. He certainly wasn't naive regarding the dangers that he would face: On the day prior to the start of war, he signed his last will and testament. A massive change in his personal life had also prompted the decision to make his will. Just three days after enlisting, his wife Juliette had given birth to their daughter, Yvonne.

Lapize was initially based near Paris, which was convenient for seeing his wife and newborn daughter, but the following year he requested a transfer to the air force. Apart from his interest in flying, airmen were often given more leave than soldiers, which may also have been one of the reasons for the transfer.

He trained as a pilot, and not long afterward was appointed as an instructor at the air base at Avord in the Cher department in the center of the country. By November 1916 he had grown tired of training and made the decision himself that he wanted to go to the front. He

Octave Lapize signed up for the Air Force during the war.

trained first as an aerial gunner at the school in Cazaux before moving to the school for aerial combat in Pau. There he learned the tactics of dogfights and also how to fly in formation.

At the outbreak of war, the Aéronautique Militaire already had twenty-one *escadrilles* (squadrons), but by October 1914 commander in chief General Barès recognized the important role aircraft would play in the escalating war and proposed that the air force be increased in size to sixty-five *escadrilles*.

Following from his training, Lapize was moved to the front in February 1917 to a base at Bar-le-Duc in the Lorraine region, where he was initially part of the N504 and N203 *escadrilles* prior to joining the N90 *escadrille* at Toul, near Nancy. The N90 was under the command of Lieutenant Pierre Weiss; members painted the fuselages of their airplanes with a singing cockerel.

Initially aircraft were predominantly used for reconnaissance work, but a French invention would radically change the role that they would play. A pilot by the name of Roland Garros mounted a machine gun on the cowling of his plane, and deflector plates to the blades of his propeller. He could thus open fire on German aircraft without shooting his own propeller to pieces.

Garros shot down an aircraft for the first time ever through a tractor propeller on April 1, 1915, but just two weeks later he was captured by Germans after crash-landing on their side of the lines. After a number of escape attempts from a prisoner-of-war camp in Germany, he eventually succeeded in 1918. He rejoined Escadrille 26, but was shot down and killed just a month before the end of the war. His name lives on, though, as a tennis center in Paris was named after him in the 1920s, thanks to his love of the sport. The Stade de Roland Garros is still the venue for the French Open every year.

In 1916 the French Ministry of War made the decision to start moving most squadrons to the area around Verdun in northeastern France. The Battle of Verdun had started earlier that year and would go on to become one of the most devastating battles of the war. An estimated three hundred thousand French and German troops were killed. Every month of the battle saw approximately seventy thousand killed, wounded, or missing in action. The Battle of Verdun lasted from February to December 1916; it was the first test of the concept of air superiority of the space over a battlefield. Lapize's squadron would remain stationed in the area after the battle.

On June 28, 1917, Lapize shot down his first German plane. Two weeks later all flights from Toul were suspended due to inclement weather. Because of the enforced time off, he took the opportunity to cycle twenty kilometers to see some friends from the N77 squadron. Despite being in combat, Lapize made use of every chance to get out training on his bike and keep in shape. One of his friends later described the encounter:

> He was really happy as he told us about how he had shot down his first Hun. He really had shot down a plane but, unfortunately, because of the altitude, the wind had taken it back behind the lines by the time it fell, too far away to be an official kill. But the champion wasn't put out, and told us it wouldn't be long before he brought down another one inside our lines. He left us in the evening, full of beans, and our last sight of old Lapize was of a figure bent over his handlebars as he sped up the hill with no apparent effort, and disappeared over the top.

Two days later, on Bastille Day, July 14, 1917, Lapize took off in his Nieuport XXIII, which bore the number 4—the same number that he had worn in his winning Tour de France. He came across a German aircraft above the woods at Mort-Mare in the commune of Flirey to the southeast of Verdun. A witness saw the battle take place at approximately forty-five hundred meters, and saw Lapize's plane being hit by the German's. His plane went into a tailspin, crashing eight kilometers from the front line. He was taken to the GAMA military hospital in Toul with severe injuries; he died there several days later. He was initially buried at the military cemetery in Toul three days afterward, where his father just managed to get there in time for the funeral.

Also attending the funeral was another famous sportsman, Maurice Boyau. Boyau had been one of the best-known French rugby players prior to the war, having helped his team, Stade Bordelais, win the French championship in 1911. He then went on to play for the French team six times, captaining them twice.

Boyau also trained as a pilot and joined up with Escadrille 77, also known as Les Sportifs due to the number of sportsmen within its ranks. He developed a reputation as one of the most successful balloon busters, which was the act of taking down observation balloons, and also was to become one of the leading French aces, with thirty-five victories. Unfortunately Boyau was also killed in action, having been shot down in the last few months of the war.

Lapize's death was mentioned in a military dispatch signed by none other than General Pétain. It was published on July 17:

Octave Lapize, an excellent pilot of unrivaled daring and bravery, having courageously engaged two enemy fighter planes, was killed on 14 July 1917, using more than three hundred cartridges in the attack.

Signed: Commander in Chief of the Eastern Armies, General Pétain

Commander of the Eighth Army, General Girard

Lapize's family later requested that his remains be transferred to the cemetery in Villiers-sur-Marne; he was reburied there in November of that year. He still jointly holds the record for most consecutive wins in Paris–Roubaix, along with Italian Francesco Moser. He was only twenty-nine years old at his death. Like many of his contemporaries, he would undoubtedly have gone on to add many other wins to his palmarès.

9

A Sense of Normality

Despite the raging war, a number of the big races in both France and Italy did manage to get organized occasionally between 1914 and 1918. It was an attempt by the authorities in those countries to bring some level of normality to the lives of citizens, and provide the populations with something positive to talk about. The French and Italian governments felt that it would be morale boosting for people who had suffered so much. In other countries involved in the war, some of the big sports tournaments would also take place. In the United States, baseball's World Series was held every year, even after the nation had entered the war. Australian Rules football would continue in Victoria, and in England the Football League played the 1914–15 season, with Everton taking the honors. It wouldn't continue after that though, as too many players signed up to fight.

In Italy, remarkably enough, the Tour of Lombardy managed to be run every year during the war, and Milan–San Remo would also

121

take place throughout the war, except for 1916. The 1918 edition of the race was won by Costante Girardengo, on roads that were said to have been in a terrible state. They hadn't been damaged from the conflict, but simply suffered from the lack of maintenance when the government concentrated on war efforts rather than the upkeep of roads.

In France several races continued away from the front. In 1916 Paris–Orléans took place as its route took riders south of the capital; it was won by the Belgian Charles Deruyter, who also took the victory in a criterium organized in Lyon that year. The following season would see five big one-day races take place in France: Paris–Tours, Tours–Paris, Paris–Bourges, Paris–Trouville, and Mont Saint Michel–Paris. A number of the Tour de France stars did manage to compete in those races. Philippe Thys won both the Tour of Lombardy and Paris–Tours in 1917 with Eugène Christophe, who was on leave from the army, in third place; Henri Pélissier took victory in Trouville–Paris. Others who were able to line up included Ali Neffati and Charles Kippert, who had both raced in the 1914 edition of the Tour de France.

It wasn't just road racing that was encouraged, though. Track racing also took place intermittently during the war, including races at the Parc des Princes and Vélodrome d'Hiver in Paris. In Germany meanwhile, where track racing was far more popular than road racing, six-day races continued throughout the war. It helped that they were so distant from the front. Even the National Track Championships were held, as well as various road races. Unfortunately Belgium was not in a position to organize any road races, although the Brussels Six-Day did manage to take place in 1915, with Belgian riders filling the top six places.

While many of the top cyclists of the era had rushed to enlist at the outset of war, others were more reluctant. It was difficult for riders to avoid becoming involved, though. Various cyclists initially avoided conscription by fleeing to the United States, which hadn't yet entered the war. In June 1917, though, it was announced that the US Congress would introduce a bill requiring that all citizens of Allied countries of military age be rounded up and handed over to their respective governments. At the time, there were cyclists from Australia, Canada, France, Italy, and Belgium plying their trade in the country. Among those who would be affected and sent back to Europe were Michel Debaets, who had been second in the 1910 Belgian championships, and Victor Linart, who won European and world titles on the track.

One man who managed to avoid part of the conflict was Henri Pélissier. On August 1, 1914, after finishing in second place in the Tour just a few days previously, he was due to take part in a track meeting at Liège. However, with rumors circulating that German divisions were ready to invade Belgium, the event was canceled. Pélissier fled for France by train, just managing to make it out before the invasion.

Pélissier was the eldest of four brothers, Charles, Francis, and Jean being the others. When war broke out, their parents pleaded with them to not enlist, but their pleas fell on deaf ears. Unfortunately tragedy struck the following year, when the youngest of the brothers, Jean, would be killed in action in March 1915 at Sainte-Menehould in the First Battle of Champagne. He had been the only brother not to become a professional cyclist; the other three all went on to become very successful. Francis was also shot twice, but managed to survive.

In 1917, while on leave from the army, Pélissier traveled to Italy to take part in the Tour of Lombardy, where he was second behind Philippe Thys. It's difficult to know whether it was due to the death of his youngest brother, or to a realization that taking part in races was a much better life than facing the enemy at the front, but by 1918 Pélissier had somehow managed to get out of the army due to his "incredibly weak constitution." This despite his ability to cycle incredibly long distances at very high speed.

Paris–Tours would take place again in 1918, and Pélissier was one of a limited number of starters. In the days leading up to the race, an article appeared in *L'Auto* outlining the challenges of even getting riders to the start line: "The entry list at Paris–Tours has stopped at 44. As we said, this is a good result and we could not have hoped for better. Military obligations, work needs in factories, and transport dif-

Henri Pélissier would get out of the Army in 1918,
and would survive the war.

ficulties have made it impossible for many other riders to register,
but our list is satisfactory, with champions like Pélissier, Thys and
Duboc." Riders were often only able to line up in races during their
periods of leave from the front.

In many ways it's understandable that Pélissier would have wanted to get away from the action: One brother had been killed, another injured, and who knows what Henri himself witnessed. After he left the military, Pélissier was also said to have been deeply affected by the death of Lucien Petit-Breton at the end of 1917. The two had been very close friends. In 1911 Petit-Breton had invited Pélissier to accompany him to Italy to take part in a number of races. It was a hugely successful trip: Pélissier took victory in the Giro di Lombardia, Milano–Torino, and Firenze–Torino–Roma. Their friendship grew from there.

Prior to 1914 he had been quite an irascible character, but after the war was over Pélissier's behavior seemed to become even more erratic. Some feel that he was seriously affected from his time as a soldier, suggesting he might have been suffering from post-traumatic stress disorder (PTSD). He definitely displayed some of the main symptoms of PTSD, anger and irritability, on numerous occasions after the war. In the 1920 Tour de France, he was penalized two minutes by Desgrange for leaving a flat tire by the roadside, so he decided to quit the race. In 1924 he abandoned the race after Desgrange would not allow him to remove a jersey. Desgrange would later describe Pélissier as "a pigheaded, arrogant champion." His home life was also said to have been very turbulent; he and his wife, Léonie, had many heated arguments. However, his irrational behavior may also have been influenced by the quantity of drugs he would later admit to having taken.

Pélissier continued to race until 1924, building up a great palmarès. Among the classics he won after the war were Paris–Roubaix, Bordeaux–Paris, Paris–Tours, Paris–Brussels, and the Tour of Lombardy again, in addition to winning the Tour de France in 1923. However, his life ended in tragedy. In 1933, a number of years after his retirement, his wife Léonie shot herself with a revolver, apparently no longer able to put up with his bizarre behavior. Two years later Pélissier would be shot dead by his new lover, Camille Tharault.

They had apparently been arguing when Pélissier lunged at her with a knife, cutting her face. She fled to the bedroom and pulled the revolver with which Léonie had shot herself from a drawer. She ran back toward Pélissier and shot him five times. The following day's *Paris-Soir* quoted Tharault as saying, "If I'd had the money I would have left him long ago."

The organizing of races between 1914 and 1918 was a valiant effort by governments and race organizers alike, but unfortunately it was just a temporary respite from the grim realities of war.

10

Death in the Skies

Octave Lapize was far from the only cyclist who would sign up for the Service Aéronautique as a pilot. It seems that it wasn't just the speed and thrill of flight that drew so many cyclists to take to the air. For some, their interest also arose from their natural curiosity about all things mechanical. It should also be remembered that the pioneers of aviation, Orville and Wilbur Wright, had gained much of their expertise from working not only with motors and printing presses, but also with bicycles. The brothers had opened a bicycle shop, The Wright Cycle Exchange, in 1892, and four years later started manufacturing their own brand. They used the income from the shop to help fund the development of their first airplane in 1903.

Seven years after the Wright brothers' inaugural flight, the world's first air force would be formed in France, the Aviation Militaire, and the following year airplanes would be used in combat for the first time, in the Italo-Turkish War. The Italians used their airplanes for reconnaissance and bombing missions on Turkish positions in Libya.

The first military use of airplanes by the French would take place in Morocco, where once again they were used for reconnaissance purposes. Even at the outbreak of the First World War the following year, there were no purpose-built fighter planes. That would soon change, though, as planes were developed with the sole purpose of shooting down the enemy's reconnaissance planes.

A very well-known cyclist, François Lafourcade, who would go on to become a pilot, was best remembered for two particular incidents. The first came in 1910, when Lafourcade became the first-ever cyclist in the Tour de France to cross the Pyrénées' famous Col d'Aubisque. The second incident—one of the most bizarre stories from those early Tours—would take place the following year.

Lafourcade was born in Lahontan, between Bayonne and Pau, in the Pyrénées-Atlantique region. His brother, Ferdinand, would also race for a time as a professional. Thanks in no small part to his diminutive stature, Lafourcade turned out to be an excellent climber. He was nicknamed The Little Pyrenean.

In his first Tour de France in 1906, where he raced as an individual, Lafourcade abandoned on the first stage. The following season he signed for the small Montabro team. His second Tour went a lot better for him, as he finished in thirteenth position overall. One of his first big results also came in 1907 when he finished in third place in the Bol d'Or track race won by Léon Georget. Lafourcade would go on to finish on the podium of the race five times without ever getting to the top step.

He moved on again to bigger and better things in 1908, when he signed for the mighty Alcyon-Dunlop team, which included more than fifty riders. There he would race alongside many of the biggest names in the sport, including Eugène Christophe, Hippolyte Aucouturier, and Louis Trousselier. He stayed with them for just one season before moving on to Biguet-Dunlop and then Panneton-Leman for the 1910 season. His new team wouldn't enter a team in the Tour that year, though, so he raced alone.

With so many big names lining up in the 1910 Tour, nobody expected that Lafourcade would be the first man to cross the Col d'Aubisque. It was the first-ever big mountain stage of the race, and Octave Lapize had been first to cross the first three big climbs, the Col de Peyresourde, the Col d'Aspin, and the Col du Tourmalet. However, Lapize was unexpectedly caught by Lafourcade on the Aubisque.

Two of the Tour organizers, Alphonse Steinès and Victor Breyer, were positioned on the climb that day, expecting to see Lapize or one of the other big names pass them first. They were very surprised, though. As Breyer wrote later:

> *And suddenly I saw him, a rider, but one I didn't*
> *know. His body heaved at the pedals, like an au-*
> *tomaton on two wheels. He wasn't going fast, but*

he was at least moving. I trotted alongside him and asked, "Who are you? What's going on? Where are the others?" Bent over his handlebars, his eyes riveted on the road, the man never turned his head nor uttered one sole word. He continued and disappeared around a turn. Steinès had read his number and consulted the riders' list. Steinès was dumbfounded. "The man is François Lafourcade, a nobody. He has caught and passed all the 'cracks'. This is something prodigious, almost unbelievable!"

Unfortunately he was caught by Lapize and others on the way toward the finish in Bayonne, but still managed to hang on for fifth. Apart from being the first to cross the Aubisque, Lafourcade was one of only three riders who managed to get over the Tourmalet that day without dismounting. He reached Paris in fourteenth position.

The second, darker incident that was most associated with Lafourcade was the poisoning of Paul Duboc, which took place in the following year's Tour, on the stage from Luchon to Bayonne. Going into the stage, Gustave Garrigou was leading the race by ten points over Duboc. It was undoubtedly the toughest stage of the race and could decide the winner. The stage was exactly the same route where Lafourcade had made his name the previous year: Riders had to climb the Col de Peyresourde, Col d'Aspin, Col du Tourmalet, and finally the Col d'Aubisque. Duboc attacked early on and gained a decent

François Lafourcade would become the first cyclist to cross
the Col d'Aubisque and would go on to become a pilot in the war.

lead. It seemed that he was going to close in significantly on the race leader, Gustave Garrigou.

It all started to go wrong for Duboc on the Aubisque, though. On the climb he started to look quite sickly and eventually fell off his bike in front of a car, which just missed him. He started to vomit, and was also suffering from diarrhea. He lay there for a long time; the rules forbade him from getting help from anybody. He was caught and passed by the other riders. His manager eventually came to his aid, and suspected something untoward. He was given an emetic to help him vomit and rid himself of the substance. He finally came around and was able to get back up and go on to finish the stage. It would later emerge that somebody had tampered with his bidon.

The first man to be accused of poisoning Duboc was Gustave Garrigou, as Duboc was closing in on his lead. Duboc's fans were up in arms, and Duboc made the declaration, "Citizens of Rouen, I would be leading the race if I hadn't been poisoned. You know what you have to do when the race crosses the city." The threat was very real. Garrigou ended up riding through Duboc's home city of Rouen in disguise. He was provided with a fake mustache and blue glasses. It worked—he was able to get through Rouen unscathed.

Despite the suspicions, it seems now that Garrigou was in fact innocent of any wrongdoing. Lafourcade was later accused of the act, and he was found guilty by the governing body of cycling in France, the Union Vélocipédique Française (UVF), which banned him for life. Lafourcade decided to take out a license with a small rival organization, La Société des Courses, with which he would go on to win both Bordeaux–Paris and Paris–Chatellerault. While Lafourcade initially denied any part in the poisoning of Duboc, he was said to have confessed some years later. He would go on to take part in seven Tours de France in total. He completed the race three times; the final time he made it to Paris was in 1912, where he was twenty-ninth.

When the war started a few years later, Lafourcade signed up to pilot bombers. The Service Aéronautique had started bombing raids as early as August 1914, when they dropped bombs on German airship sheds at Metz using Voisin III aircraft. The bomber squadrons would also attack Freiburg railway station and a poison gas factory at Ludwigshafen in those early months of the war, with limited success.

On August 10, 1917, Lafourcade was involved in an operation with his squadron, Escadrille 485, under the command of Lieutenant Maurice Moch. They had started patrols of the English Channel earlier that year, and that day had seemed like another routine operation. On their return to their aerodrome at Eu beside the coast, however, Lafourcade's airplane caught fire two hundred meters above the ground. Fire was possibly the greatest fear that World War One pilots had, as any break in gasoline lines that developed into fire would set the wooden and canvas planes alight in seconds. Many pilots whose planes caught fire were found to have shot themselves rather than burn to death, while others decided to jump. One British pilot, Arthur Gould Lee, wrote in his memoirs: "What a way to die, to be sizzled alive or to jump and fall thousands of feet. I wonder if you are conscious all the way down. I'd much prefer a bullet through the head and have done with it."

Lafourcade chose to jump, and died upon impact with the ground. His gunner, Auguste Plurien, was also killed. In the last year of the war the Germans would outfit their pilots with parachutes, but they were the only air force to do so. The design of cockpits made no allowance for the space required for a bulky parachute, and high commands of the various air forces would not consider a change. If one had been available, a parachute may have saved Lafourcade's life.

A remarkable aviator from the First World War who had tried to take part in the Tour de France was Marie Marvingt. She had gained her pilot's license in 1910, and was also an avid sportswoman. She had tried to enter the 1908 Tour, but the organizers refused because of her sex. Yet Marvingt decided to cycle the route regardless—and not only that, but she would complete it, whereas only 36 of the 114 men who had officially entered the race had made it back to Paris. Marvingt was also a skilled mountaineer and would be the first woman to climb many Alpine peaks in addition to winning numerous competitions in a range of sports, including the bobsledding world championships.

When the war started, Marvingt would disguise herself as a man and enlist with the French army. She first served on the front with the Forty-Second Infantry Battalion, and when she was discovered, she signed up to fight with the Italian army instead. After fighting in the Dolomites, she enlisted in the air force and received the Croix de Guerre for the bombing missions she flew over Germany. She survived the war, and her life of adventure would continue right up until her death at the age of eighty-eight. In the 1950s she was flown over Nancy in northeastern France in a US fighter jet; two years before her death she cycled from Nancy to Paris.

In Belgium an early pioneer of aviation was Aimé Behaeghe, who also happened to be a racing cyclist. Both Aimé and his brother Joseph took up cycling at a young age, and at eighteen Aimé finished in eighth place in the 235-kilometer Liège–Bastogne–Liège of 1909, ahead of the likes of Philippe Thys. That year he also finished in second place in Etoile Caroloregienne, won by Paul Deman. He really had the makings of a top-class cyclist, but decided to concentrate on aviation instead.

He and his brother built their own airplane, which they completed in 1910, and they started to build them for others, too. In 1913 they moved to Brazil to work as pilots for their postal service, but returned home when war broke out. Aimé volunteered for the Belgian air force, while Joseph signed up for the infantry. Aimé served in Belgium for the first year of the war, flying numerous missions over the front before being transferred by the Belgian Ministry of Colonies to the Force Publique in the Belgian Congo.

There he was assigned to pilot seaplanes on Lake Tanganyika, where the Belgians hoped to take control of the full lake from the Germans in German East Africa. It was a long and difficult campaign, in which Behaeghe played a significant part. Not only did he become one of the first pilots in Central Africa, but he had also helped assemble the airplanes upon arrival in Belgian Congo. Unfortunately he died of dysentery in the small town of Niemba in the Katanga province at the end of 1916.

Understandably, air accidents would account for the deaths of many pilots in the war. Airplanes, were after all, a new invention, and designers were still learning how to make the machines more robust and reliable. Two well-known cyclists were killed in the same accident—Léon Hourlier and Léon Comès. Hourlier was a track cyclist who had been French champion three times and also won the Grand Prix of Paris in 1912 and 1914. Together with his brother-in-law, Comès, they won the Paris Six-Day in 1914. Comès would also finish in second place in the Brussels Six-Day, where he partnered with Lucien Petit-Breton.

When the war started, Hourlier was assigned to the army and initially worked as a driver. However, he felt he would be of better service to his country as a pilot. In February 1915 he requested a transfer to the air force, and his request was granted. After two months training at the Aviation Academy at Alvor, he was moved to the front.

The track cyclists Léon Hourlier and Léon Comès would
die tragically in the same accident.

Among his missions were the bombing of railway lines and factories
at Saarbrucken. He would be awarded the Croix de Guerre.

On October 16, 1915, Comès and Hourlier decided to pay a visit
by airplane to meet up with another sportsman who was also a pilot,
Georges Carpentier. Carpentier was a boxer who had become both
European middle- and lightweight champion before the war, and
during the war would be awarded both the Croix de Guerre and the
Médaille Militaire. He would survive and go on to become the world
light heavyweight champion in 1920.

Unfortunately both Comès and Hourlier died when the airplane,
which was being piloted by Comès, nose-dived and fell from the sky

near Coperly, southeast of Reims. The cause of Comès and Hourlier's crash was never established, but it was suspected that their propeller had fallen off.

Another cyclist who would die in an airplane accident was Henri Alavoine, the younger brother of the more famous Jean Alavoine. Henri competed in four Tours de France, his best finish coming in 1913 when he was twenty-fifth—but given a small number of finishers, he also happened to be last overall. He struggled the following year, only managing to finish in fifty-second place and third from the last. Alavoine wouldn't be the only last-place finisher to die during the war. His brother Jean, meanwhile, had a very successful Tour, finishing in third place overall. He'd already won six stages of the race by the time war broke out.

Henri was killed on July 19, 1916. His plane at crashed near Pau, and although he survived the impact, he subsequently died in the hospital. Jean would survive the war and continue to race until 1925, winning seventeen stages of the Tour in total.

A rider who had finished nine places ahead of Alavoine in the 1914 Tour was Emile Guyon. Despite being Swiss, Guyon signed up to fight for France at the start of the war, enlisting at Besançon. He, too, became a pilot, but died in an accidental plane crash at Pau in October 1918. The list goes on and on. Albert Delrieu was shot down by a German plane; Emile Quaissard was killed in a dogfight. The Germans weren't immune, either, with one of their best road riders,

Franz Gregl, also killed in a dogfight. Piloting was indeed a dangerous occupation. Pilots of the Service Aéronautique claimed 2,049 enemy aircraft during the war, but at a massive loss: An estimated thirty-five hundred pilots were killed in action, three thousand went wounded or missing, and another two thousand were killed in accidents.

However, one positive outcome from the numerous aviation accidents was that great advances were made during the four years of the war, allowing for much safer postwar civil flights. But this came at a great price.

11

The Italian Front

The images of the trenches in Belgium and France spring immediately to mind when many people think about the First World War; it can often be forgotten that the war was fought on numerous other fronts. Battles also took place in Africa, the Middle East, and even the Pacific.

One well-known cyclist would even die in Pakistan, in an indirect conflict associated with the war. Herbert Gayler had competed for Britain in the 1912 Olympics in Stockholm, where he finished thirtieth in the road race and won a silver medal in the team event. When the war had started, Britain decided to bring some smaller conflicts it had been involved with to an end, so as to concentrate efforts on the war back in Europe. Shortly after the start of the war, Gayler enlisted with Twenty-Fifth County of London Cyclist Battalion, and in 1915 he was sent to Pakistan. Two years later there was a revolt among Mahsud tribesmen in the west of the country in Waziristan.

The British were able to restore calm to the region, but local tribes didn't trust the British and rejected their peace proposals. Local militia would launch further attacks on the British troops. It was during one of these attacks that Gayler was hit by rifle fire during an ambush in a valley near Kotkai Bozi Khel. He later died of his wounds.

Back in Europe, an Eastern Front emerged a few weeks after the start of the war once Russia had invaded East Prussia and the Austro-Hungarian province of Galicia. The front stretched all the way from Latvia to Hungary. In May 1915 another front opened in northern Italy when Italy declared war on Austria-Hungary and Germany.

The intention of the Italians was twofold: They wanted to block the threat of an Austrian advance into the Trentino region around Lake Garda, and also to push toward Trieste in the east. One of the first and most important points that the Italian troops seized control of in those first few days after the declaration of war was the Stelvio Pass. The pass—which was built by the Austrians back in 1825—stands at 2,757 meters and is one of the highest in the Alps. At the time it formed the border between the Austro-Hungarian Empire and Italy. In more recent decades the Stelvio has become one of the most iconic climbs of the Giro d'Italia, even though it wouldn't be used until 1953.

As had been seen in France, numerous professional cyclists also took up the fight for Italy. The sport had also became extremely popular in the early decades of the twentieth century, with many big races established. The Giro d'Italia had started just a few years before the onset of war in 1909, after the editor of the newspaper *La Gazzetta dello Sport* suggested the idea to the owner of the paper, Emilio Costamagna. The Tour de France was the inspiration for the race, as Costamagna had seen how beneficial it had been for *L'Auto.* In addition, *La Gazzetta* had already created two other bike races that had proven successful: Milan–San Remo and the Giro di Lombardia.

Milan–San Remo was first organized in 1907; Lucien Petit-Breton took that year's victory. The Giro di Lombardia was a little bit older, first run in 1905. The 1912 edition of the race was won by a twenty-three-year-old cyclist from just north of Milan, Carlo Oriani, when he managed to outsprint his compatriot Enrico Verde and Frenchman Maurice Brocco at the finish in Milan.

Oriani had been born in the commune of Cinisello Balsamo on November 5, 1888. He started work at an early age in nearby Sesto San Giovanni, which had become the home of many industries, finding work as a stonemason. He also developed an interest in cycling around this time, and he used to split his time between work and the bicycle. He initially raced as an independent but in 1909 signed for the Stucco team.

The Giro di Lombardia in 1912 had been the big win that Oriani had been looking for. He had come close before, having finished in second place in the Coppa del Re and fifth in the Giro d'Italia in

1909. The following year he was second on a stage of the Giro, just ahead of Lucien Petit-Breton. Winning the Race of the Falling Leaves meant that he would go into the following year's Giro as one of the favorites. However, following his win in Lombardia, Oriani signed up for the Italian army, which was fighting against the Ottoman Empire. The Italo-Turkish War—or the Guerra di Libia, as it was known in Italy—had started at the end of September 1911 when Italian troops invaded Tripoli.

Oriani had enlisted in the distinctive corps known as the Bersaglieri. Formed back in 1836, this was a light infantry unit known for wide-brimmed hats and also for the fact that members jogged on parade rather than marching. To enable even faster movement, the Bersaglieri decided to start using bicycles. In 1913 they asked the bicycle manufacturer Bianchi to produce a machine for their troops. The design that they arrived at had some unique features, including optional mounts for a machine gun, rifle, or parts for a mortar. The bikes could also be folded to enable easy transport and had solid tires to limit the likelihood of punctures. Twelve cycling battalions would be used by Italy during the war.

Despite not cycling while he was serving his country, Oriani had managed to keep himself somewhat fit. He was released from service at the start of 1912, which enabled him to take part in that year's Giro. After so long away from the bike, though, Oriani was clearly out of form. On the first stage from Milan to Padova, he struggled and was left behind early on by the leaders. He resorted to taking a shortcut but was caught and disqualified from the race. He vowed never to become involved in a similar situation and trained with extra determination thereafter.

The following year's Giro would start in Milan, where the ninety-nine riders who had signed up faced an opening stage of 341 kilometers to Genoa, via Turin. Among the favorites to take the overall victory were Carlo Galetti, who had won the previous three editions, and the 1909 winner Luigi Ganna. After his absence from the sport, nobody really fancied Oriani to take the win in what would be the last edition of the Giro d'Italia to be run with a points system.

On the opening stage the first man, Giuseppe Santhià, arrived home after twelve hours, with Oriani finishing in a disappointing eighth position. Due to the race being run on a points system, it didn't really matter how near or far behind the winner Oriani was; it was his position on the stage that was key. He would have to improve a lot to take the overall honors in Milan. Two days later the race headed south to Siena in Tuscany. Oriani finished the stage in fifth to move up to seventh place on General Classification, seven points behind the leader, Pierino Albini.

Oriani made more progress up the leader board as the race moved farther south. After the fourth stage, to Salerno, he had moved up into third place, ten points behind Giuseppe Santhià from Piedmont. It was still a big gap to overcome, though. His bid for glory received an unexpected bonus on that fourth stage when one of the pre-race favorites, Carlo Galetti, was forced to retire after breaking his foot. The fifth stage proved disastrous for race leader Santhià, who could only manage thirteenth and slipped down to second overall. Oriani remained in third place, eight points behind the new leader, Eberardo Pavesi.

Oriani was incredibly consistent throughout that Giro despite not claiming any stage wins. The leadership changed hands again before Oriani took over after the penultimate eighth stage to Rovigo, with a slender two-point lead over Giuseppe Azzini. Oriani would have to be vigilant on the last stage over 321 kilometers to Milan. The stage was won by Pavesi with Oriani in second. He ended up winning the Giro by six points from Pavesi, who had leapfrogged over Azzini into second. Not only had he won the Giro, but he became the first-ever Grand Tour winner to go through the race without winning a stage. An estimated hundred thousand fans witnessed his triumph at Parco Trotter in Milan.

Oriani returned to defend his Giro title the following year. The 1914 race would be the first time that the General Classification was based on time, and in the system that we are familiar with today, each rider would have his finishing time totaled for all stages to determine the overall leader. Eighty-one riders started the race that year, but in what has been arguably called the hardest Grand Tour ever, only eight would go on to finish.

The Giro d'Italia winner Carlo Oriani would sign up for
the famous Italian corps, the Bersaglieri.

Once again the race started in Milan. Oriani—who had moved to the Bianchi-Pirelli team by this time—was seventh on the opening stage to Cuneo in the Alps, which included the climb to Sestriere. The race was run off in atrocious conditions, and only thirty-seven riders made it through that first stage. Two stages later Oriani was third behind Costante Girardengo on the longest-ever Giro stage, over 430 kilometers from Lucca to Rome. That was as good as it got for Oriani, though, and he would be among the majority of riders who retired in awful conditions. The race was won by Alfonso Calzolari, who finished almost two hours ahead of the second-place finisher, Pierino Albini.

Despite the outbreak of war a few months afterward, the Giro organizers were confident that it would not affect Italy and went ahead with planning for the 1915 edition. However, their plans were scuppered when the Italians entered the war just before the Giro was due to start, on May 23. Soon after Italy declared war on Austria-Hungary, Oriani returned to the Bersaglieri.

Carlo Oriani was far from being the only Italian cyclist to see action in the war. Ottavio Bottechia from the Veneto region also served with the Bersaglieri. He had grown up near what became the front with Austria-Hungary, and due to his local knowledge spent much of the war bringing messages and supplies among various towns in the region, as well as among trenches.

He had started his working life as a forester but, looking for more adventure, would later join the army. Apparently one of the officers in his battalion saw him one day hauling a heavy machine gun up a mountain on his bike, and said to him, "You know, you ought to be a racing cyclist, not a soldier." When he finished his military service he went on to race professionally.

Botecchia wasn't just involved in messenger duties during the war, however; he also saw action at the front. He was said to have displayed considerable courage throughout the war and was in 1917 awarded with a medal for bravery: "Calmly and bravely under violent enemy fire he returned fire efficiently and in a deadly manner with his own machine gun, inflicting serious damage on the enemy and stopping their advance. Forced on numerous occasions to retreat, he ignored the danger and carried his weapons with him so that he was able to open fire again and again."

Bottechia later recalled an incident from his service: "I was to take the machine gun to a lookout post that was under heavy fire. I had to ride on paths and animal tracks which were steeper than those of the Galibier or the Izoard. I arrived at my destination later in the evening after a risky alpine climb. The next day I found my efforts had not been in vain. The Austrians attacked in the night and had failed to take the post thanks to the new machine gun."

In 1922 Bottechia made the decision to turn professional, racing for the Ganna-Dunlop team in France, and winning a stage of the Tour the following year. Bottechia would go on to become the first

Italian winner of the Tour de France in 1924, and repeated the feat
the following year. Unfortunately he died just a couple of years later
in mysterious circumstances. In 1927 farmers found Bottechia lying
by the roadside with a cracked skull and numerous broken bones.
His bike lay nearby but was undamaged. There was nothing to suggest that he had been hit by a car.

Ottavio Bottechia would survive the war, and
go on to win the Tour de France in 1924 and 1925.

He was taken to hospital but died twelve days later, having never
regained consciousness. Rumors abounded as to how he had met his
end. One story was from an Italian man who lay dying on the streets
of New York years later from stab wounds. He claimed that he had

been employed as a hit man to kill the champion cyclist. Another man, a local farmer, claimed that he found Bottechia eating his grapes and, enraged, had thrown a large stone at him, hitting him on the head.

Oriani, meanwhile, would be with the Bersaglieri when they fought at the Battle of Caporetto in 1917. The battle took place from October 24 to November 19, near the town of Kobarid on the Austro-Italian front. In August that year, the German general Paul von Hindenburg recognized that they needed to show Austria-Hungary support to keep the empire in the war. He devised a joint operation between the two forces with the intention of inflicting severe damage on the Italian army.

The Austrians and Germans launched their attack at 2 AM on the twenty-fourth, catching the Italian army by complete surprise. The battle started with an artillery barrage, followed by the launch of poison gas. German and Austro-Hungarian infantry then launched an assault on the Italian line—which in certain sections they were easily able to breach. The Italians were in disarray, trying to contend with the overpowering enemy forces.

The Italians initially tried to hold their line, but eventually they were forced to retreat west to the Tagliamento River; the decision came on October 30 that they should retreat to the far side of the river. The German and Austro-Hungarian armies were closing in fast, but it would take the retreating army a full four days to cross the wide

Tagliamento. Fortunately for the Italians, though, the enemy advance had been so rapid that their supply lines were stretched, and the immediate danger was gone.

The breathing space gave the Italians time to retreat farther. By November 10 they had established a position at the Piave River. By the time the Germans and Austro-Hungarians reached the Piave, severe fatigue and hunger had set in. The Italian troops were in the stronger position, and were able to push their enemy back at the Battle of the Piave River.

Yet this victory was little consolation for the events that had taken place the previous week: The Battle of Caporetto had been absolutely disastrous for the Italians. An estimated ten thousand troops had been killed and another thirty thousand wounded. In addition, 265,000 Italian soldiers surrendered to the Austrian forces.

Oriani was supposed to have been among the men placed at the riverbank to help defend the area and allow soldiers to cross the river. Some reports suggest that they came under enemy fire, and Oriani was forced to jump into the river's icy waters. Other reports indicate that Oriani jumped in to try and save a drowning comrade. Regardless, Oriani nearly drowned in the currents of the fast-flowing river, though he eventually managed to reach the western bank. Unfortunately, enduring the bitter temperatures in wet clothes took its toll on Oriani, who he developed a fever a few days later. He was taken to hospital, where he was diagnosed with pneumonia. His health deteriorated, and by early December it was clear that he would not recover. His wife was summoned and just managed to arrive at his bedside before he slipped away on December 3.

The following year an eighteen-year-old American by the name of Ernest Hemingway would also become involved in the conflict in Italy. Hemingway had volunteered for the Red Cross.

Although he was not involved in the Battle of Caporetto, where Oriani lost his life, Hemingway described it in one of his most famous novels, *A Farewell to Arms*. The description given by Hemingway in the chapter titled "The Retreat from Caporetto" seems to accurately describe the withdrawal of troops from the action and the escape across the Tagliamento that Oriani endured. It suggests that Hemingway had spoken directly to men involved in the retreat across the river.

> *I looked at the carabinieri. They were looking at the newcomers. The others were looking at the colonel. I ducked down, pushed between two men, and ran for the river, my head down. I tripped at the edge and went in with a splash. The water was very cold and I stayed under as long as I could. I could feel the current swirl me and I stayed under until I thought I could never come up. The minute I came up I took a breath and went down again. It was easy to stay under with so much clothing and*

my boots. When I came up the second time I saw a piece of timber ahead of me and reached and held on with one hand. I kept my head behind it and did not even look over it. I did not want to see the bank. There were shots when I ran and shots when I came up the first time. I heard them when I was almost above water. There were no shots now. The piece of timber swung in the current and I held it with one hand. I looked at the bank. It seemed to be going very fast. There was much wood in the stream. The water was very cold. We passed the brush of an island above the water. I held onto the timber with both hands and let it take me along. The shore was out of sight now.

La Gazzetta dello Sport launched a campaign to earn funds to transport Oriani's body back home, and after a few months enough funds were raised. Vast numbers flocked to his funeral in Sesto San Giovanni, just to the south of Cinisello Balsamo, where he had grown up. He was buried in the neighboring cemetery.

The Italians would eventually turn the course of the war in October 1918 with victory at Vittorio Veneto. It marked the end of the war on the Italian front, but at a tremendous loss. An estimated 650,000 Italians died in the war, and the economic impact on the country would last for years; in turn this fueled Benito Mussolini's rise to power. The Italians did gain most of the territories that had been promised to them if they helped the Allies to victory. Among the areas awarded to Italy was South Tyrol, where the Stelvio Pass is located. It meant that the pass would be entirely in Italy rather than bordering Austria.

The Giro d'Italia resumed in 1919 and was won by Costante Girardengo, the man who had competed in his one and only Tour back in 1914. As with the Tour de France, that year's Giro peloton would struggle to cope with the conditions of the roads in the north of the country, which had been destroyed during the war. Only fifteen of the sixty-one starters made it to the finish in Milan.

On the second stage of the race from Trento to Trieste, the peloton would have to cross the River Tagliamento, where Oriani had struggled and developed pneumonia. It was somewhat apt that his fellow cyclists would also struggle to cross the river: A bridge that had been blown up during the war was still awaiting repair, and riders had to cross by foot. No doubt the memory of Oriani was at the forefront of many of the cyclists' thoughts that day.

12

The Elegant Argentinean

One of the more remarkable stories that emerged from the first few months of the war was an incident that was to become known as the "taxis of the Marne," and among those involved in the operation was the first double winner of the Tour de France, Lucien Petit-Breton. The battle that the action was part of was considered by many to have altered the course of the war.

The massive German offensive aimed toward Paris as part of the Schlieffen Plan had reached the River Marne by early September. After just five weeks of the war the German army was within a hundred kilometers of Paris. This prompted a high level of anxiety among the French populace; the French army even placed demolition charges on all the bridges over the Seine.

The German army hoped to break through the French defenses, and by early September, French generals realized that their Sixth Army was on the verge of collapsing. More troops were needed at the front, but there wasn't enough military transport available to get them there. With this in mind, General Joseph-Simon Gallieni, the military governor of Paris, decided to commandeer six hundred cars, including many of the city's taxis, to help transport six thousand reserve infantry troops to the front line. When told that their taxis were being used for the mission, some of the drivers asked about reimbursement. They were told they would receive 27 percent of the meter reading.

The convoy of mainly Renault AGs departed from the Esplanade des Invalides in the seventh arrondissement, not far from the Eiffel Tower, at 10 PM on September 6. They loaded four men with full kit inside each car; a fifth man stood on the running boards of the car.

En route the convoy collected more soldiers from the 103rd and 104th Infantry Regiments on the other side of Paris. Petit-Breton and the other drivers drove without headlights to the villages of Nanteuil-le-Haudouin and Silly-le-Long, sixty kilometers northeast of Paris, where they dropped off the troops. Many of the drivers then turned around again to collect more soldiers from Paris. Two infantry regiments of Zouaves, who had recently arrived from Tunis, were among those ferried by taxi.

Gallieni had famously said upon seeing the fleet of taxis ferrying troops to the front, *"Eh bien, voilà au moins qui n'est pas banal!"* ("Well, here at least is something out of the ordinary!") Many historians credit Gallieni for having saved Paris from the Germans, rather than Marshal Joseph Joffre, the general in charge of the army. Even the commander of the German army, General von Kluck, would later say, "There was only one general, who against all the rules, would have dared to carry the fight so far from his base; unluckily for me, that man was Gallieni."

Most historians agree that the contribution of the taxi drivers to the actual battle was minimal, but the effect on the morale of the French troops was immense. For the soldiers already on the front who were under huge pressure, it was a relief to see reinforcements arriving and realize that they hadn't been forgotten. The story would also be used afterward for propaganda reasons. However, following from the battle, the conflict would descend into trench warfare for the next four years, resulting in a huge loss of life. After the operation on the Marne, Petit-Breton would continue to spend much of his time in the war ferrying officers to and from the front.

The 1907 and 1908 Tour winner wasn't always known as Lucien Petit-Breton, though. He had been born Lucien Georges Mazan in Plessé in what was then Brittany, but is now in the Loire-Atlantique *département*, in 1882. His father Clement was a clock maker by trade and had developed quite a successful business. However, he had also developed a deep interest in politics and decided to run in the parliamentary elections when Lucien was just a young boy. He ended up losing the election by a massive margin; in turn, he also lost many of his customers. He was thoroughly humiliated. Around this time, the Argentinean government was looking for skilled immigrants; needing a change, Clement decided to uproot and move to South America.

Clement sailed to Argentina along with his wife Desirée, but left Lucien and his brother Paul, who was three years older, behind in the care of their aunt Felicity, the sister of Desirée. Their mother would return to France two years later to collect her two sons and bring them to Argentina. By this time Clement had established a clock repair business in a French section of Buenos Aires. Not long after they arrived back in Argentina, Desirée gave birth to a third son, Anselme; three more children would also arrive over the next few years.

Their father was a hard taskmaster, and all of the children would be made to start work at a young age. When he was fourteen, Lucien started working in the most luxurious hotel in Buenos Aires, the Jockey Club, which had been founded by future Argentine president Dr. Carlos Pellegrini. Two years later he won a bicycle in a lottery; he soon took up racing at the city's velodrome. He was a natural and would go on to become Argentinean track champion while still a teenager.

However, his father thought his interest in cycling was a waste of time and compared racing on the track to being a circus clown. He wanted his son to concentrate on his real job. So out of fear of his name appearing in race results, Mazan started using his pseudonym, which came about accidentally. He said later, "So the first time I raced, without my parents knowing of course, I was asked my name and I hesitated. I said, 'Breton, I'm a Breton.'" He was explaining where he was from, but the organizers took it as his name. He would later change his alias to Petit-Breton to avoid confusion, as when he moved to France, he found out that there was another cyclist called Lucien Breton.

Despite having moved to Argentina, at the age of twenty Petit-Breton was conscripted into the French army. After serving his time, he stayed on in the country of his birth and took out an independent racing license. He initially just raced on the track, where he would wear Argentinean colors. The young rider was very successful there,

The 1907 and 1908 Tour winner Lucien Petit-Breton
rests during a six-day race.

winning the prestigious twenty-four-hour Bol d'Or track event, among other races. Still, Petit-Breton really came to prominence in 1905 when he switched his attention to the road. He was signed by the J. B. Cycles team, and he made his Tour debut that year, finishing in a remarkable fifth place overall.

Not long afterward he took on the challenge of the world hour record, which had first been set by Henri Desgrange back in 1893. The test was to cover the longest distance within one hour, and he was trying to take the record from Willie Hamilton who had covered 40.781 kilometers on the track at high altitude in Colorado Springs back in 1898. Petit-Breton would make his attempt at the Vélodrome Buffalo in Paris. The stadium—built in 1893 near Porte Maillot in the western suburbs of the city—had been named after Buffalo Bill Cody, who had set up camp there. It was demolished in 1915 to make way for an airplane factory. For much of the record attempt, it was unclear whether Petit-Breton would succeed, but he managed to cover 41.110 kilometers to beat Hamilton by just over three hundred meters. He would hold on to the record for just two years, as another Frenchman, Marcel Berthet, would increase it by another 410 meters.

Petit-Breton was signed by the Peugeot team for the 1906 season and improved on his Tour performance that year, when he finished in fourth place overall; he also won his first big one-day race, Paris–Tours. The following year he would claim victory in another classic at the start of the season, this time in Italy when he won the inaugural edition of Milan–San Remo.

Petit-Breton's first Tour win later that season was fortunate to say the least. Although he was in great form, there was one man was head and shoulders above the rest of the competitors that year. Émile Georget had won four of the first seven stages in addition to placing second on two of the others. That year's race comprised fourteen stages, totaling 4,488 kilometers, and Petit-Breton did get stronger as the race progressed. Still, halfway through the race, Georget appeared to have an unassailable lead.

Then on the ninth stage, from Toulouse to Bayonne, it all fell apart for Georget. He crashed at a checkpoint but was relatively uninjured and able to go on. One of his Peugeot teammates, Pierre-Gonzague Privat, gave him his bike—and that was the problem. The Tour rules of the time stated that a rider must start and finish on the same bicycle. When news of the offense emerged, Georget was demoted to last place on the stage with forty-eight points. He dropped from leading the race to third place overall. Petit-Breton, who had won the stage after attacking alone with two hundred kilometers remaining, became the new leader, while Georget's hopes of a Tour victory all but disappeared.

As harsh as Georget's penalty had seemed, the rival Alcyon team felt that the organizers hadn't gone far enough in penalizing him. The *directeur sportif* of their team, Edmond Gentil, had wanted Georget kicked out of the race. When Desgrange ignored his protests, Gentil withdrew the entire team from the Tour.

Petit-Breton now led the race by fifteen points over Gustave Garrigou, and he consolidated his lead by winning the eleventh stage from Bordeaux to Nantes. Garrigou and Georget won the next two stages, but Petit-Breton was second both times, and on the final stage to Paris he finished third to win the race overall.

It was a popular win, as Petit-Breton was very well liked by the public. He wasn't known just for his strength on the bike, but also for his stylish dress sense and appearance. He would later become known as simply "The Argentine" or sometimes "The Elegant Argentine" due to his sartorial elegance. Henri Desgrange was to say of Petit-Breton, "He has an amazing split personality because this slim young stylish man, reserved, charming and cultivated becomes a raging demon on his bicycle." His charm helped him to gain attention from many admiring women, and one in particular caught his eye. He would go on to ask Marie-Madeleine Macheteau, the daughter of a hatter, to marry him.

Despite his great results on the road, he still raced on the track when the opportunity arose. One such race was the New York Six-Day in December 1907. He and with a number of other top Europeans were invited to compete against the best American cyclists. However, Petit-Breton didn't perform as well as he had expected against the track specialists.

The ship that he had sailed on across the Atlantic for the event would play a prominent part in the war. It ended up being refitted for troop transportation at the start of hostilities. The SS *La Provence* was ultimately torpedoed and sunk by a German U-boat on February 26, 1916.

A number of newspaper reports of the sinking said, "Captain Vesco remained on the bridge, calmly giving orders, before finally shouting, 'Adieu, mes enfants.' The men clustered on the foredeck, and replied, 'Vive la France.' Then the *Provence* made a sudden plunge, and the foredeck rose perpendicularly above the water. A British patrol and a French torpedo boat picked up the survivors after they had been 18 hours in the water. Many died or went mad before the rescue ships arrived." It was estimated that nearly a thousand were killed in the sinking.

While it could be claimed that Petit-Breton's victory in the 1907 Tour was fortuitous, the same couldn't be said about his win in 1908. In addition to winning the race overall, he also won five stages. His teammates François Faber and Georges Passerieu completed the podium, but were thirty-two and thirty-nine points behind Petit-Breton.

That year's race followed nearly the same route as the 1907 Tour, and 114 riders lined up at the start. Petit-Breton had started that year's race as the clear favorite, as that season he had already added another classic to his palmarès, Paris–Brussels; he had also dominated the Tour of Belgium where he won four stages and the overall. A change for the 1908 Tour was that Desgrange required all riders to race on bikes provided by the organizers. Petit-Breton lived up to this billing as Tour favorite, finishing second on the opening stage to Roubaix, five minutes behind Passerieu. Two days later on the second stage to Metz, he outsprinted Passerieu to move alongside his teammate at the head of General Classification.

His skill as a bicycle mechanic also enabled Petit-Breton to ensure his status as favorite: The rules at that time said that cyclists had to repair their bicycles without help. This could be crucial in the event of any mechanical difficulties. A report from the time outlines his fastidiousness regarding looking after his bicycle:

> *Slender in build, apparently of not more than average physique, Petit-Breton was a fine example of what can be done by a cyclist possessing determination and method. He was practically his own trainer, and would never allow an outsider to touch his machine, the condition of which is a matter of supreme importance in the one-month's Tour de France, which must be accomplished throughout on the same bicycle. Frequently, after a 200-mile road race, he would have his machine carried up to his bedroom, and carefully clean it and adjust it himself in readiness for the next stage of the race. Perhaps*

more than any other French cyclist, Petit-Breton pos-
sessed grit. The more strenuous the conditions and
the worse his luck, the more determined he appeared
to become, and many a competitor who thought he
had shaken off Petit-Breton for the entire race was
disagreeably surprised to find him come up strong
at the end.

Petit-Breton moved into the lead by a massive fifteen points on the third stage, which crossed the Ballon d'Alsace climb in the Vosges Mountains. Nobody threatened his lead after that; he would go on to win another four stages to end up with five stage wins out of a total of fourteen stages. He had been utterly dominant, and his Peugeot team had managed to win all of the stages.

His first prize for winning the race was four thousand francs, and he also won the first-ever mountain competition in the race, Le Prix Labor-Hutchinson. Afterward, Petit-Breton, always conscious of the support from his sponsors, said of his win, "I never doubted my victory for one moment. I was marvelously well prepared. I knew I could count on Peugeot and my Lion tires; in short, I won comfortably enough, even though I met some men who made my life difficult." He didn't outline who these men were.

His popularity in France grew even more, and in the months after the race he published a book titled *Comment je cours sur route* (*How I Ride the Route*). The book was a success, and he started to write

Lucien Petit-Breton was involved in
ferrying French troops to the Battle of the Marne.

columns for newspapers. He wasn't universally popular, though, and did have his detractors. He had been so dominant in that year's race that rumors started to circulate that he had been using drugs. He strenuously denied the charges. "It has been said I owe my greatest victories to drugs. Allow me to contest these absurd rumors. Do you seriously think a man, however strong, could survive such treatment for twenty eight days?"

The use of drugs in the early years of the Tour de France was written about in a remarkable article by the journalist Albert Londres, which appeared in *Le Petit Parisien*. *"Les Forçats de la Route"* was written after an interview with Henri Pélissier and his brother Francis, following on from their disqualification from the 1924 Tour.

> *"You have no idea what the Tour de France is,"*
> *Henri said. "It's a Calvary. And what's more, the*
> *way to the cross only had 14 stations—we've got 15.*
> *We suffer on the road. But do you want to see how*
> *we keep going? Wait . . ."*
>
> *From his bag he takes a phial. "That, that's co-*
> *caine for our eyes and chloroform for our gums . . ."*
>
> *"Here," he said, tipping out the contents of his*
> *bag, "horse liniment to keep my knees warm. And*
> *pills? You want to see the pills?" They got out three*
> *boxes apiece.*
>
> *"In short," said Francis, "we run on dynamite."*

Henri takes up the story. "You ever seen the baths at the finish? It's worth buying a ticket. You go in plastered with mud and you come out as white as a sheet. We're drained all the time by diarrhea. Have a look at the water. We can't sleep at night. We're twitching as if we've got Saint Vitus's dance. You see my shoelaces? They're leather, as hard as nails, but they're always breaking. So imagine what happens to our skin. And our toenails. I've lost six. They fall off a bit at a time all through the stage. They wouldn't treat mules the way we're treated. We're not weaklings, but my God, they treat us so brutally. And if I so much as stick a newspaper under my jersey at the start, they check to see it's still there at the finish. One day they'll start putting lumps of lead in our pocket because God made men too light."

It has been well documented that many different drugs were used by cyclists in those early years, including strychnine, cocaine, alcohol, and ether, so it seems reasonable that the question was asked of Petit-Breton. He avoided any more questions on the issue, though, and at the end of that season he had more reason to celebrate: On November 24 Petit-Breton married Marie-Madeleine Macheteau in the church in Vallet in the Lower Loire.

Petit-Breton would also participate in the Giro d'Italia three times.

He took part in the very first running of the race, in 1909, but crashed out on the first stage from Milan to Bologna. He returned in 1910 race with the Legnano team and 1911 with Fiat, but despite not finishing either race, he did have some good placings. He also managed a stage win in 1911 in Turin, and he really impressed some of the Italian journalists, who wrote of his pedaling style in glowing terms. That stage win was to be his last major victory. He left the sport for a time, and established a bike shop in Périgueux in the Dordogne region. He did return to racing, though, soon afterward.

Remarkably enough, despite starting the Tour numerous times after his second win, he would never manage to finish the race again. He didn't enter the race in 1909, but instead followed the race as a columnist for a newspaper. He would end up abandoning the race every year from 1910 through to 1914. He suffered some terrible luck in these editions, though. In the 1911 race a rider sitting in front of Petit-Breton swerved to avoid, of all people, a drunken sailor. Petit-Breton collided with the swerving rider and ended up in hospital and out of the race.

He did come close to victory in the 1913 edition, though. Going into the penultimate stage of the race from Longwy to Dunkirk, he was in second place overall behind the Belgian Philippe Thys. However, he crashed badly on that stage and was forced to withdraw. The following year he raced with the Automoto-Continental team, alongside Costante Girardengo and Paul Duboc. His best results were ninth and tenth on two particular stages, but again he ended up abandoning for family reasons.

Within days of hostilities being declared, Petit-Breton had signed up to serve his country again. He served with a transport unit, the Twentieth Escadron du Train des Équipages Militaires (ETEM). The Twentieth ETEM had been formed back in 1875, and had served all around the world, in Tunisia, Indochina, Madagascar, and Morocco, among other places.

The year after the First Battle of the Marne—Petit-Breton had been involved—the Mazan family suffered its first tragedy when Lucien's younger brother was killed. Anselme Mazan had also raced professionally. He took part in the 1904 Bol d'Or, and he lined up alongside his brother for the Peugeot team in the 1907 Tour. However, he abandoned on the seventh stage on his one and only appearance at the race. His best result was probably twelfth in the 1909 Grand Prix Wolber. Anselme had become a pilot at the start of the war, and was killed in a dogfight above the Bois de la Gruerie in the Argonne on June 8, 1915. Lucien's eldest brother, Paul, also raced professionally, and in 1908 he would win the Volta Ciclista Tarragona. Fortunately, he would survive the war.

Petit-Breton tried as best he could to overcome the death of his brother, and he continued his service with the army. Two years later, on December 20, 1917, he was driving twenty kilometers from the front near Vouziers in the Ardennes when he was involved in an accident. A drunken butcher with a horse-drawn cart moved into his path. In the darkness he didn't see the horse and cart on the road until it was too late, and he collided with it with considerable force. His car turned over. Petit-Breton was thrown from the car while his traveling companion escaped unscathed.

The great champion was taken away from the front to the hospital in Troyes, but he was already dead. There was much sadness about the death of the popular Petit-Breton among cycling fans when the news was reported in newspapers over the following days. Petit-Breton wouldn't be the only cyclist with Argentinean links to be killed in the war. Georges Cadolle was born in Buenos Aires in 1889, and had raced for the Alcyon-Dunlop team alongside Gustave Garrigou and Octave Lapize, among others. He also signed up for the French army and died on August 2, 1916, at Cerisy Gailly near the Somme.

Petit-Breton was buried in a cemetery in Pénestin, beside the Atlantic coast, not far from where he was born. His son Yves went on to become a professional cyclist, and then a successful *directeur sportif.* He managed the France West team in the 1948 Tour de France, and would also manage the Peugeot team.

Petit-Breton's name has never been forgotten, though, as a velodrome was opened in Nantes in 1924 in front of ten thousand spectators and named in his honor. An Argentinean Olympic delegation would later erect a monument there in his name, and the velodrome is still used to this day.

13

The Youngest Rider

In June 2013 nineteen-year-old Dutch cyclist Danny van Poppel became the youngest cyclist to take part in the Tour de France since the Second World War. In doing so, van Poppel helped bring attention to the youngest-ever Tour entrant, Camille Fily, who had taken part in the most controversial Tour ever, in 1904. Fily, who was dubbed "The Lochois Kid" by journalists, was just seventeen years and fifty days old when he took to the start line that year. He took the record from another seventeen-year-old, Jean-Baptiste Zimmermann, who had taken part in the very first Tour. At the opposite end of the scale, there was also a fifty-year-old taking part, Henri Paret. A decade after his debut Tour appearance, Fily would also see action in the First World War.

Fily was born on May 13, 1887, in the small village of Preuilly-sur-Claise, south of Tours, in the Indre-et-Loire department. His start in cycling came when he joined his local club, the SV Lochoise. Despite his record-breaking feat of being the youngest Tour rider, he wasn't the most famous cyclist from his village. Léon Georget, "The Father of the Bol d'Or," also came from there. Georget earned his moniker from winning the famous Parisian track race nine times, in addition to winning Bordeaux–Paris twice. Léon's younger brother Émile also won Bordeaux–Paris as well as nine stages of the Tour de France. Both brothers would survive the war.

Fily quickly made an impression on the bike. He was enthralled by the reports from the first-ever Tour in 1903, and vowed that he would also take part in the race. His opportunity came the very next year, when his entry was one of those accepted by the organizers. Eighty-eight riders lined up at the start of the second Tour on July 2, but this number would be quickly cut down: Thirty-three of the riders pulled out on the first stage, from Montgeron to Lyon. Fily was among those who managed to survive that first stage. He avoided any trouble on the second stage when supporters of local rider Antoine Fauré, who was from Lyon, attacked many of his rivals. The Italian rider Giovanni Gerbi was particularly badly beaten, having been knocked unconscious and suffering a broken finger. He was forced to abandon.

On the third stage, from Marseille to Toulouse, Fily finished sixth, twenty-five minutes behind Hippolyte Aucouturier, and had another top-ten finish on the penultimate stage from Bordeaux to Nantes. Now he wasn't just surviving; he was showing that he was worthy of his place alongside the older, more experienced riders. There was more trouble on that second-last stage, with nails being thrown on the road, and more scuffles involving supporters. Shots had to be fired at Nîmes to disperse one mob. Numerous riders were also being disqualified by Desgrange after stages for various infringements. Riders were accused of getting lifts in cars and taking illegal feeds. In addition, there were instances of bikes being sabotaged. The race had become a farce.

On the last stage of 462 kilometers from Nantes to Paris, Fily tried a daring attempt to win the stage. He broke away in darkness at Saumur, not far from his home village of Preuilly-sur-Claise. By Tours his lead was up to seventeen minutes and by Amboise—twenty-five kilometers later—it was up to twenty-five minutes. At the halfway point, though, he really started to struggle and was caught by Blois. Fily did go on to finish the stage, albeit four hours behind.

This result left him in ninth place overall in Paris, fifteen and a half hours behind the victor, Maurice Garin. However, the win left a bad taste. Such was the amount of cheating and violence during the Tour that Desgrange considered pulling the plug on the race. He published an article in *L'Auto* the following day titled "The End": "The Tour de France has just finished and its second edition will, I fear, be the last. It will have died of its own success, of the blind passions which have been unleashed, of the abuse and the suspicions that have come from ignorant and ill-mentioned people." Desgrange would soon have a change of heart on the future of the race, however, saying that he had "decided the show would go on, once more as a moral crusade for the sport of cycling."

With his winnings from the race, Garin bought a petrol station shortly after the end of the Tour. However, he didn't have much time to bask in the glory of his win. In November of that year the UVF decided to launch an investigation into the result. Complaints had been received from a number of cyclists about the amount of cheating that had taken place. During the race nine riders had been disqualified for using cars and trains.

The UVF listened to testimony from many competitors, and after considering all the evidence released their findings on December 2. They had decided to disqualify all of the top four finishers—Maurice Garin, Lucien Pothier, César Garin, and Hippolyte Aucouturier. This meant that Fily had now moved up to fifth place overall.

Unfortunately further investigations took place, and other riders would be disqualified, including Fily. In total, twenty-nine riders were ousted, but the reasons were in most cases never made clear. Some of the punishments dished out were severe. Lucien Pothier, who had originally finished second, was banned for life; the original race winner, Maurice Garin, was banned for two years. His crime was to accept food outside the official feeding zone. By contrast, in the 2013 Tour de France race leader Chris Froome would also take food outside of the permitted feeding zone and receive a twenty-second penalty.

Henri Desgrange was livid with the investigators, for two reasons: first, that the UVF had undermined him by handing out additional penalties to the riders, even though he had already penalized them; second, that it had taken the UVF so long to hand out the penalties. He wrote in *L'Auto*, "It is extremely difficult to establish whether the heavy punishments handed out by the UVF to the principal riders were motivated by serious reasons, when we are given only the results of these decisions while at the same time the documents which they used are withheld from us. It is no exaggeration to say that public opinion will demand from the *Union Vélocipédique* some explanation, which will no doubt be forthcoming."

Unfortunately the UVF didn't provide the explanation that Desgrange demanded. The 1904 Tour really highlighted one of the problems the organizers faced with stages as long as they were. Four of the six stages in that race were more than four hundred kilometers in length, and even at the height of the summer this required much of the racing to take place at night. Riders would often take advantage of the darkness to engage in various methods of cheating. Desgrange's helpers tried their best to keep an eye out for underhanded tactics, but it was very difficult to keep track of so many riders over such long distances.

Henri Cornet was awarded the victory four months after the race finished; like Fily, he was still just a teenager. Just shy of his twentieth birthday, Cornet remains the youngest winner of the race. Apparently even he had cheated during the race, getting a lift in a car at one stage. Cornet would retire from cycling just prior to the start of the war. Meanwhile the original race winner, Maurice Garin, continued to protest his innocence for years afterward, telling anybody who would listen that he was the real victor of the race. This was despite claims against him that he had not only taken illegal feeds, but also hopped on a train at one stage.

Unfortunately the altered results of the race meant that Fauré, whose supporters had violently attacked other riders on Stage 2, was now awarded the victory for that stage. It would be his one and only stage win.

The events left a black mark on the race, and despite many more scandals since, the 1904 is still the closest the Tour has come to stopping for good. It was absolutely farcical. Despite his early reservations, Desgrange actually started planning the following year's race soon afterward, albeit without many of the big names, who would still be banned. Fily was also suspended for a while, but he would return in time for the 1905 Tour in good form. Just prior to the start of the race, he had a good result when he was tenth in Bordeaux–Paris, won by another of the suspended riders, Hippolyte Aucouturier.

Fily's main motivation for the 1905 Tour was to make amends for the previous year's disqualification, and clear his name. Despite being still only eighteen years old, he put in an incredible performance.

Racing for the Guerin Cycles team, Fily had three top-ten stage plac-ings, and finished in fourteenth place overall; Louis Trousselier took the victory. It was to be Fily's last appearance in the race. Despite showing such great potential, he retired from cycling at the end of the year. His reasons are unknown.

Little would be heard of Fily until the following decade when war broke out. He had signed up to fight in 1915, and was assigned to the Eightieth Infantry Regiment. This regiment fought with great distinction at Ypres in 1914, and at Champagne and Verdun in the following years. In 1918 they would face the Germans again near Ypres. In April of that year General Ludendorff drew up plans for the Germans to retake Ypres. The plan, known as Operation Geor-gette, had the objective of driving the British forces back to the Eng-lish Channel ports and forcing them out of the war.

After four years of fighting, many of the troops on the Allied side were war-weary and low on morale. The initial attacks by the Ger-mans as part of the operation would see a number of British and Por-tuguese divisions collapsing. On April 17 the First Battle of the Kemmel took place. Here the German Fourth Army tried to take over the strategically important Kemmelberg but was repulsed by the British. However, there was a very real danger that the Germans would capture it if there was another offensive.

The Kemmelberg was important for both sides: At 156 meters in elevation, it overlooked much of the area surrounding Ypres. The

German soldiers near the Kemmelberg in 1918.
The climb is a key feature in Ghent-Wevelgem.

same week that the British repulsed the Germans, Marshal Foch agreed to send French troops including Fily's Eightieth Infantry Regiment to the Lys sector, where the hill was situated. After the initial British defense of the Kemmelberg, it was agreed that the rested French troops would relieve the British of the position.

On April 25 the Germans attacked again, and this time they were successful in capturing the Kemmelberg. Fighting would continue in the area until the end of July, and casualties would mount for both sides. Two weeks after the Germans had captured the hill, on May 11, Fily was carrying a message by bike at Millekruis, just to the north of the Kemmelberg, when he was shot. He died instantly, just two days before his thirty-first birthday.

Every year thousands of fans converge on the Kemmelberg to witness the riders tackle the climb used in Ghent–Wevelgem, and it is the main focal point of the race. Ghent–Wevelgem was first organized in 1934 as a race for amateurs, and would only have a professional version after the Second World War. On the climb, the cyclists race past Le Mont-Kemmel French Military Cemetery. There is also an eighteen-meter-high statue commemorating the sacrifice, the *Monument aux Soldats Français*. The cemetery contains the bodies of 5,237 unknown French soldiers and 57 whom the authorities did manage to identify. It would have been some consolation to Fily's family that his body could be identified. His body wasn't interred on the Kemmelberg, but instead was returned to his family, and he would be buried at the military cemetery in Loches, just south of Tours, near where he had been born.

Fighting would continue in the area, and the Kemmelberg was retaken by British, French, and American troops in September. The death toll in the area would continue to rise throughout the year. The number buried in the cemetery on the Kemmelberg is but a drop in the ocean compared with the number that died in the Battle of the Lys. An estimated thirty thousand French soldiers were killed along with eighty-six thousand German and eighty-two thousand British. The sacrifice of the Allied soldiers had made a difference, though: The Battle of the Lys would cause considerable damage to the German army and mark the beginning of the end of the war.

In 2014 the organizers of Ghent–Wevelgem would pay homage to those who died on the Kemmelberg by routing the race past a number of the larger war cemeteries, as well as the Menin Gate, where the names of so many missing men are engraved. In addition to being honored for the sacrifice he made in the war, Fily will also be forever remembered for his cycling achievements. His record of being the youngest-ever Tour entrant is one that will probably stand the test of time.

14

Lanterne Rouge

Each year in the Tour de France a distinction is bestowed on the rider who finishes in last place. The rider is deemed to be the *Lanterne Rouge;* the name is taken from the lantern that used to hang on the back of trains in France. The lantern would allow station masters to see that no carriages had come uncoupled from the train.

One such man who is listed as being one of the very first *Lanternes Rouge* of the Tour is Georges Bronchard, who would take the honor in the 1906 race. What is remarkable about his finishing position is that although he was very last, he still managed to finish in fourteenth place—such was the attrition in that year's race. Ninety-six riders had started the race that year, so finishing fourteenth out of that many competitors sounds considerably more impressive than finishing last.

Bronchard was born in Fontainebleau to the south of Paris on January 21, 1887, and would race as a professional cyclist for just four years, competing in the Tour de France in three of those years.

Ironically enough, the Tour where he was *Lanterne Rouge* also happened to be his best finish. In 1907 he finished in twenty-first place, and the following year, he was twenty-ninth. In 1909 he joined the Le Globe team, where he counted Lucien Pothier—who had finished in second place in the 1903 Tour—as one of his teammates.

Seventy-six riders started the 1906 Tour, and because Bronchard was not a member of one of the big teams, he would race alone, being sponsored by the bicycle manufacturer Biguet. He was in good form coming into the race: Not long beforehand, he had finished in tenth place in the epic Bordeaux–Paris, even though he was still a teenager. This augured well for his debut in the Tour. Unfortunately his chances of a high finish disappeared on the opening stage to Lille, as he came home in a disappointing thirty-eighth position, three hours and forty-two minutes behind the stage winner, Émile Georget. It went from bad to worse for him on the next two stages, as he came in eight hours and twenty-two minutes down on the second stage to Douai. On Stage 3 the riders would have to negotiate the Ballon d'Alsace, and Bronchard came in more than nine hours behind the stage winner, René Pottier. At least he had cycled the distance. Four riders were disqualified when it was found out that they had taken the train.

The General Classification was based on points rather than time, so the fact that Bronchard was arriving so long after the leaders didn't affect his standing overall. However, it cannot have been good for his

Georges Bronchard arrived in hours behind the leaders
on nearly all of the stages of the 1906 Tour.

morale to be continuously so far behind the leaders every day. Also,
the extra time that he was spending on the bike was cutting into his
resting time. Bronchard was extremely resilient, though, and as others
dropped out, he persevered.

Pottier, who had previously won both Paris–Roubaix and Bordeaux–Paris, seemed to be running away with the race: After five
stages he was nine points ahead of Georges Passerieu. On the stage
over the Ballon d'Alsace, he had broken clear alone and stayed away
for two hundred kilometers to win the stage, forty-seven minutes
clear of Passerieu. However, Passerieu was dogged and would win the
following seventh stage, beating Pottier by three places to reduce the

gap to five points. That was as close as it got, though. Pottier won the final stage to finish eight points clear and make it five stage wins out of eight.

Unfortunately Pottier's life would end in tragedy. He never really showed any outward signs of happiness, even after his various successes, and he appeared to be suffering from depression. In January 1907 he hanged himself from the bike hook in his shed. The reasons why the incredibly gifted climber made this decision are unclear. One story holds that he was distraught after learning that his wife had been having an affair while he had been taking part in the Tour the previous year. Desgrange would later erect a statue on the Ballon d'Alsace in his memory, the scene of his greatest victory.

So Bronchard was among the few who made it to Paris, and was deemed to be the *Lanterne Rouge.* However, it turned out that Bronchard's daily struggle to make it to the stage finish may not have been the tough slog it had first appeared. He was accompanied on many of the stages by another rider, Leon Winant. In an interview with *L'Auto,* Winant was asked why he and Bronchard were always the last riders to arrive. He said they "were in no hurry." Indeed, they seemed to be more interested in availing themselves of as much free food along the route as they could than they were in actually racing. The duo would sing to spectators as they passed through cities, and Winant would show off by descending with his feet on his handlebars. The duo got slower as the race went on; on the penultimate stage from Brest to Caen, Bronchard's average speed was an incredibly low thirteen kilometers per hour.

In subsequent decades the title of *Lanterne Rouge* would develop a considerable amount of cachet, resulting in the farcical situation of riders in the final few days of the Tour fighting to finish last. The reason was that the *Lanterne Rouge* could command some substantial contracts in the post-Tour criteriums, whereas nobody remembers who comes second last in the race.

In the 1979 Tour the two riders sitting in the last and second-to-last positions were within one minute of each other coming into the last few days. One of them, Philippe Tesnière, knew the value in coming last, having done so the previous year. Thus he and the other rider, Gerhard Schönbacher, rode extra slowly in the final time trial. They were the two slowest riders that day, but Tesnière had gone overboard. He was outside the time limit and was kicked out of the race. The following year, the Tour organizers would introduce a rule whereby in the last week of the race, the rider sitting in last position each day would be kicked out of the race.

The post-Tour criterium circuit hadn't been established back in 1906, so unfortunately Bronchard was unable to exploit his *Lanterne Rouge* title. In his final Tour in 1909, he retired on the very first stage from Paris to Roubaix. He left racing soon afterward, without having made a significant impact on the sport.

When war broke out a decade later, Bronchard signed up in

Fontainebleau and was assigned to the Section d'Infirmiers Militaires of the Third Army as a stretcher bearer, dealing with the dead and seriously wounded from countless battles.

In the final year of the war his battalion was stationed at Villers-sur-Coudun, just north of Compiègne. In April 1918 a report emerged from that village, while Bronchard was stationed there, that at first might not have seemed particularly significant—but it was. Documents in the Archives du Services de Santé des Armées show that the first case of influenza on French soil had appeared in the Third Army. It would turn out to be Spanish flu. Within weeks the British soldiers based in France would also report outbreaks of flu. The disease had been first reported in the United States in February. Apparently American troops who had arrived in Bordeaux in April, and were dispatched to the front soon after, had brought it with them.

The first wave of the flu didn't kill many but did cause considerable weakness in the army. A week after the first reports emerged, on April 27, Bronchard was wounded in battle. He was attended to by medics before being taken away by ambulance. Unfortunately he died on the way to hospital. The exact details of his injuries are unknown—only that he died of his wounds in Ambulance Number 247. He may well have taken a shot while attending to somebody else who was already wounded.

Following from the identification of Spanish flu in Bronchard's battalion, a second wave would appear the following month. This would be considerably more severe and affect the French and other armies badly. A massive number of troops would be hospitalized. One of the most remarkable aspects of the Spanish flu was that it was more deadly among healthy young adults than it was children or the elderly—the groups more often most vulnerable. In this case, however, nearly half of the fatalities would be of individuals between the ages of twenty and forty. It has been speculated that this may have been a result of the immune systems of healthy young adults over-responding to the threat of infection with the small proteins known as cytokines.

Three weeks before the end of the war the influenza outbreak would claim the life of another famous cyclist. Georges Parent from near Aix-les-Bains in the Alps was a three-time world champion at the motor-paced event on the track from 1909 to 1911. Parent had also enlisted in the French army at the start of the war, and ended up being wounded a number of times in battle. On October 22, 1918, just weeks before the Armistice was signed, he succumbed to the flu. It was estimated that between two and four hundred thousand people were killed by the Spanish flu in France in the space of just a few months. Bronchard and Parent were among the last of the professional cyclists to die in the war.

It's difficult to determine the total number killed by the flu world-wide, but estimates range between fifty and one hundred million, or up to 5 percent of the world's population. It was felt that troops' close proximity to one another, coupled with the massive troop movements during the war, contributed to the rapid spreading of the virus. That malnutrition had weakened the immune systems of soldiers and civilians alike may have been another factor.

A Canadian professor, Dr. Andrew Price-Smith, who is an expert in pandemic influenza, has hypothesized that the virus helped swing the outcome of the war in favor of the Allies. He has suggested that the flu affected German and Austrian troops considerably more than it did British or French. Whatever the reason for the change of fortunes, after four long years it seemed like the war was finally coming to an end.

15

Sentenced to Death

In 1913 Belgian journalist Karel van Wijnendaele organized a race that would become one of the monuments of the sport. Van Wijnendaele wanted the Tour of Flanders to rival the big one-day race in the French-speaking part of the country, Liège–Bastogne–Liège. The first edition of *De Ronde van Vlaanderen* on May 25 of that year attracted just thirty-seven riders. It passed through most of the big towns and cities in Flanders before finishing in Mariakerke, a suburb of Ghent.

At Mariakerke, after 324 kilometers, participants raced four laps around a small lake on a narrow track. Apparently one of the riders was so exhausted that he fell into the lake. The victory went to a twenty-four-year old from West Flanders: Paul Deman—born in Rekkem, just a few hundred meters from the French border—took the win ahead of two other Flandrians, Joseph Vandaele and Victor Doms. The race really captured the imagination of the Flemish peo-

Paul Deman became the first winner of the Tour of Flanders in 1913.

ple. Deman said afterward, "In all my life I never saw so many people as on the first day of the Tour of Flanders. Everywhere along the road they were there in their thousands."

Flemish cyclists would dominate the race for decades, due in no small part to the fact that it was held on the same day as Milan–San Remo, which attracted the best Italian riders and many of the best French.

Deman had first made a name for himself in 1909 when he dominated the amateur Tour of Belgium, winning six out of the seven stages. Unfortunately the only stage he didn't win was the one finishing in his hometown. The prize money enabled him to help purchase a house for his parents. Deman gave up his job as a carpet maker to turn professional the following season, and made his Tour de France debut in 1911, where he finished an impressive thirteenth place overall.

Later on in the season Deman would just miss out on a stage victory in the Tour; he finished second to his compatriot Marcel Buysse in Perpignan. He ended up in fourteenth place overall in Paris. The following year Deman took another big victory, this time winning the epic 592-kilometer Bordeaux–Paris, ahead of his teammate and the man who had beaten him in Perpignan the previous season, Buysse. Deman would have another crack at the Tour that summer, lining up for the Alcyon-Soly team. He had a great start, finishing in sixth place on the first stage; after three stages he was in seventh place overall. However, that was as good as it got, and he soon abandoned the race.

When war broke out shortly afterward, Deman would continue to train, but with an ulterior motive: He was working as a courier for the intelligence services, carrying messages around Belgium and also across the border into the Netherlands, apparently in a gold tooth. The work was highly dangerous—he risked death if he was caught. After fourteen successful missions, Deman's luck finally ran out in November 1918 when he was stopped by the Germans, who found the message he was carrying.

Deman was just one of many involved in the Belgian underground resistance movements. One of the most successful networks established during the war was La Dame Blanche, which had over a thousand members. It was organized by a British agent named Henry Landau, who had established various imaginative ways of documenting and transmitting information on troop movements. Beans were used to indicate the numbers of soldiers on trains passing through the country. Messages were carried in hollowed-out broom handles, in bars of soap, and sewn into clothes.

Also involved was Anna Lowyck, who was caught in 1915 near the Dutch border when she was trying to pass information on the German U-boat base near at Zeebrugge. She avoided execution and would spend the duration of the war in various German prisons. One of the first to be executed was August Succaud from Bruges, who had

In 1918, Deman was captured by the Germans
and sentenced to death.

been providing information about German military installations that were later shelled by the British. He was killed by firing squad in December 1914. In 1917 thirteen members of another network, the De Pauw group from Waregem, were executed for providing the British with information about German troop movements.

Deman was arrested and jailed in Leuven, east of Brussels. The Germans charged him with espionage, and a trial was quickly organized. Hundreds had already been executed throughout the war for spying for Belgium, so his chances of survival seemed slim. The German court did find him guilty and sentenced him to death. Often those found guilty would face the firing squad the very next day. Fortunately for Deman, the Armistice was signed while he was awaiting execution. However, his joy would soon turn to frustration.

The British army had taken over the prison at Leuven and took an interest in Deman. He spoke with a strong West Flandrian accent, which they didn't recognize as Flemish. Believing him to be a German instead, they decided to proceed with the execution anyway. Before they could go through with it, a letter came from the Belgian authorities proving his identity, and Deman was eventually released.

His bravery was recognized by the French after the war, when he was awarded the Croix de Guerre. Deman made a successful comeback to cycling after the war, and would continue his winning ways in the classics, beating Eugène Christophe and Lucien Buysse in the 1920 Paris–Roubaix. Three years later he won Paris–Tours.

After retirement, Deman moved to Outrijve, where he would establish a bicycle factory. He later moved to nearby Avelgem, where he was undoubtedly an inspiration to one of his neighbor's children. The young boy, Marc Demeyer, would also go on to win Paris–Roubaix in 1976. Deman died in 1961 at the age of seventy-two, but his feats have never been forgotten. In 2013 he was remembered by the Tour of Flanders organization. They chose his hometown of Rekkem as the Dorp van de Ronde. Every year, a different village on the course of the Tour of Flanders is put in the spotlight, and numerous festivities take place. One hundred years after his victory, it was Deman's turn to be remembered.

16

Armistice

In the first half of 1918 the war appeared to be swinging in the Germans' favor. By June they were in control of more territory than they had been since the onset of hostilities. Despite their advances, however, the tide started to turn for them very quickly in the middle of the year, for a number of reasons. The British naval blockade was making it difficult for them to obtain supplies, for one thing; in addition, the United States entered the war in 1917 to bring new momentum to the Allies.

A famous American cyclist who became involved in the conflict was Bobby Walthour. He had won world championship track titles in 1904 and 1905, and competed successfully on both sides of the Atlantic. Before the war he participated in quite a few six-day races in Berlin and Frankfurt, among other places, and decided to open up a bank account in Germany for his earnings. Unfortunately for Walthour, during the war Germany decided to seize any foreign-held bank accounts, and his savings were taken from him. Perhaps this was his motivation for joining the war effort. He joined the YMCA in the United States and after undertaking training himself, moved to France for the last few months of the war to help teach fitness to French soldiers.

The US entry into the war brought more and more fresh troops into the conflict. After the failure of a number of offensives that year, morale in the German army was also rapidly dropping.

The Allies made considerable advances against the Germans in August, even though they were outnumbered by forty-two divisions to thirty-two. That month the Allies captured their objectives on the Western Front on nearly a daily basis. On the Eastern Front, nearly four hundred thousand Austrians had deserted their army by September. The two chiefs of the German forces, Field Marshal Hindenburg and General Ludendorff, realized that victory in the war was now impossible, and they persuaded Kaiser Wilhelm II that a cease-fire was needed. Negotiations started between the Germans and the Allies at the forest of Compiègne on the morning of November 9, 1918.

The agreement that was drawn up was based on the Fourteen Points peace proposal devised by the US president Woodrow Wilson earlier in the year. After two days of negotiations and some final work on some of the last details, the German delegates signed the agreement at ten past five on the morning of November 11, 1918. The

The Armistice was signed in Marshal Ferdinand Foch's
private train carriage.

Armistice was signed in the railway carriage of French marshal Ferdinand Foch in the forest of Compiègne, near the Somme, which would later become the start town of Paris–Roubaix. A telegram was immediately sent by Foch to all Allied commanders: "Hostilities will cease on the entire front November 11th at 11.00 am French time."

Fighting would needlessly continue to the very last minute, though, as it was later established that even on the day the Armistice was signed, 2,738 men died on both sides. Many more would also die of their injuries after Armistice Day. An estimated 28,600 war-related military deaths occurred in France after the war.

Pierre Stabat, who had raced in the 1914 Tour as an *isolé* (he abandoned on the first stage of the Tour), was among those who would die of his injuries after the Armistice. Stabat passed away in December. Georges Tribouillard, who had raced in that year's Tour with the La Française–Hutchinson team, would also die from injuries after the Armistice had been signed. Tribouillard had previously finished in second place in the French cyclo-cross championships, and he finished in seventh place in Paris–Roubaix in 1911. In the 1914 Tour he abandoned on the third stage. He had been seriously injured in a plane crash during the war, and died on March 16, 1919. He was the last known cyclist victim of the war.

More than nine million combatants had been killed over the four years, with civilian deaths totaling over six million. It has been estimated that approximately 1.4 million Frenchmen were killed in action. Many more were left disfigured or suffering from post-traumatic stress disorder. There were also countless widows and children left without a father.

A formal state of war would exist between the protagonists for another seven months after the signing of the Armistice, but the fighting was over. War would formally end with the signing of the Treaty of Versailles the following year. The treaty was signed in the Hall of Mirrors at the Palace of Versailles, near Paris. Prior to the signing, French prime minister Georges Clemenceau wanted to ensure that France had more protection, saying, "America is far away, protected by the ocean. Not even Napoleon himself could touch England. You are both sheltered; we are not." Having lived through both World War One and the Franco-Prussian War, Clemenceau was particularly fearful of Germany. It was even rumored that he had asked that when he died, he was to be buried on his feet, facing Germany. Clemenceau's fears would come to fruition two decades later.

Much of Europe had been decimated during the Great War, especially when fatalities from the Spanish flu were added in to the totals. It has been estimated that fifteen million people died during the war, and up to sixty-five million people worldwide from both war and flu in those few years. There are also millions of unrecorded victims—those who lost fathers or husbands, those who returned with debilitating injuries, and those who were mentally scarred, suffering from shell shock. Thousands of widows from France and elsewhere would travel to the Western Front after the war, searching for their loved ones in vain. There were so many soldiers with severe injuries that a National Union of Disfigured Men would be established. France was one of the countries that had suffered most, with only Russia and Germany exceeding its casualty numbers.

It would be an injustice to not make reference to the numerous German cyclists who were killed during the war. Bruno Demke, a track cyclist from Berlin who had won the Grand Prix of Europe in 1910, died when he crashed his plane during takeoff on August 24, 1916, at Döberitz, twenty-five kilometers west of his home city. He had previously earned the Iron Cross when he was shot during another flight, but managed to limp his airplane back over the enemy lines.

A very recognizable name killed during the war was Ludwig Opel—the son of Adam Opel, founder of famous German automobile company. Opel was the youngest of five brothers who had raced on the track; he won the silver medal for the amateur sprint at the world championships in Vienna in 1898. He died in action in 1916 in Hungary.

Other well-known German cyclists to be killed in action included Albert Eickoll, who had won the Frankfurt Six-Day; Jacob Esser, another six-day rider; and Fritz Finn, who died in Lithuania in 1915 had raced at the Vel d'Hiv before the war and had represented Germany in the world championships.

A number of German road cyclists were also killed. Ernst Franz had won the Rund um Köln in 1913 and was killed in action in the Battle of the Carpathian Passes between a combined Austrian-German force and the Russian army. Richard Dottschadis, who won the 1912 Halle–Potsdam–Halle, died of appendicitis while in service. Many of these Germans would have raced against the top French cyclists of the time; instead, after 1914, they were forced to fight a war against each other. With the cessation of hostilities, cyclists from around Europe would once again have the opportunity to come together in the name of sport.

However, despite the Armistice, the peace in Europe was very uneasy. Twenty-two years later, Germany would invade France again. The Germans would occupy much of the country until 1944, and more than half a million French people were killed. Like the Great War, World War Two also saw the involvement of many professional cyclists from that era. Among them would be a number of Tour de France winners. Fausto Coppi would fight for the Italian army in North Africa before being captured and held as a prisoner of war, and a teenage Louison Bobet was said to have carried messages for the French resistance. The winner of both the 1938 and 1948 Tours de France, Gino Bartali, helped the Italian resistance by carrying messages while supposedly out training. It would also later emerge that he had helped Jewish families escape persecution from the Nazis.

Like many of the cyclists who fought in the first war, both Coppi and Bartali could justifiably have argued that they could have enjoyed considerably more victories but for the outbreak of hostilities. Bartali won both the Giro and the Tour prior to 1939, while Coppi also won the Giro before joining the Italian army. Once again, professional cycling would cease during those years, with the first post–World War Two Tour de France taking place in 1947. From then the sport would grow from strength to strength, however, and that postwar era is seen by many as the golden age of cycling.

17

A New Beginning

In 1919 the cycling world would try to pick up where it had left off. Although some professional races were organized during First World War, the vast majority were canceled because the three main cycling countries of France, Belgium, and Italy were so heavily involved. Less than two months after the signing of the Armistice, the newspaper *Le Petit Journal* announced that it was establishing a new bicycle race to commemorate the war; the route was to pass some of the great battlefields of the Western Front.

The Circuit des Champs de Bataille would start on April 28 and cover two thousand kilometers over seven stages before finishing on May 11. It was due to start and finish in Strasbourg and cover a route mostly in the north and northeast of the country. It would travel through a number of cities that had been affected by the conflict or threatened with invasion, including Paris and Amiens.

The start town of Strasbourg was in Alsace—a region that would be ceded back to France a few months after the race, as part of the Treaty of Versailles. The opening 275-kilometer stage to Luxembourg was won by Oscar Egg, who had taken part in the 1914 Tour. Because his home country, Switzerland, was not involved in the war, Egg was in a better position than most to retain a decent level of fitness. The race was ultimately dominated by Belgian Charles Deruyter, though, who won three stages along the way to overall victory. The French cyclists would struggle in the race, with Jean Alavoine the only one to take a stage win. It was a sign of things to come: French cycling would suffer for a number of years following the war.

Another race organized in the months after the cessation of hostilities was Paris–Roubaix. The route would take the riders through some of the most devastated areas of the Continent, as they would cross the River Somme en route to Roubaix. It was ambitious to even contemplate holding the race. The state of the roads was such that one journalist termed the race the "Hell of the North." It's a name that's still used today to describe the epic classic.

Reports of the devastation around Roubaix at the time referred to the stench of raw sewage and rotten cattle pervading the air, and the landscape being a scene of blackened tree stumps and mud everywhere. A report from *L'Auto* described the scene: "We enter into the center of the battlefield. There's not a tree, everything is flattened! Not a square meter that has not been hurled upside down. There's one shell hole after another. The only things that stand out in this churned earth are the crosses with their ribbons of blue, white and red. It is hell!"

There were many notable names missing from the start list, including previous winners Octave Lapize and François Faber, but the race would still see the likes of Philippe Thys, Oscar Egg, and Eugène Christophe taking part. Two men managed to get away from the rest, Thys and Henri Pélissier, although a delay at a level crossing enabled Honoré Barthélémy to catch them. Pélissier was easily able to out-sprint the other two at the end. He would win again two years later. It was an indication of the how scarred the landscape was that out of forty support vehicles following the riders, only five would make it to Roubaix. Pélissier said at the finish, "This wasn't a race. It was a pilgrimage."

The terrain over which Paris–Roubaix takes place still has count-less reminders of the conflict that took place last century: Cemeteries, memorials, and even trenches dot the landscape of northern France. Munitions are still being found in Belgium and France; in recent years the Paris–Roubaix route had to be changed when a huge cache of mustard gas containers was discovered.

Across the border in Belgium, the Tour of Flanders was also or-ganized that year. The race was won by Henri "Ritte" van Lerberghe, and the story of his victory is quite extraordinary. Van Lerberghe had just finished service with the Belgian army when he arrived at the

Henri Pélissier at the start of Paris-Roubaix in 1919,
with a heavy French Army presence in attendance.

start line in Ghent; he had to borrow a bicycle. He had the told the
other riders that he would ride them all off his wheel, and to their
amusement he attacked soon after the start. They allowed him to
gain a gap, but had clearly underestimated his strength: His lead grew
and grew. By the time the peloton realized how far behind they were,
his lead was unassailable.

However, coming toward the velodrome at the finish, Ritte
stopped at a local pub to order a beer. He decided to have another,
and then a few more. His coach eventually located him and had to
persuade him to leave the pub and finish the race. At this point van

Lerberghe was too inebriated to cycle. He resorted to walking his bicycle around the track at the finish. His lead had been reduced to fourteen minutes, but he did hang on to win.

Three months after the Tour of Flanders, the Treaty of Versailles was signed on June 28, 1919, ending the state of war between Germany and the Allied Powers. The following day, the first postwar Tour de France started just ten kilometers away at the Parc des Princes. Desgrange had been working on the route since the end of hostilities.

It had only been seven months since the end of the fighting when the Tour restarted, so many of the riders did not have too much time to train. Most went into the race underprepared. To compound their difficulties, Desgrange in his infinite wisdom also decided to make the 1919 Tour 5,560 kilometers in length, the longest to date; only one Tour since has been longer, in 1926.

There were to be a number of significant changes to that first postwar Tour. For the first time organizers would provide cyclists with food for the race; previously participants had looked after themselves. It was one less thing for them to have to worry about in a time of shortage. Another major change was the introduction for the first time of the yellow jersey. And as had been seen at Paris–Roubaix earlier that year, the state of the roads constituted a major difference from prewar tours. Many of the roads had been badly damaged or even destroyed; this made the going really difficult for both cyclists and those following in cars.

Life was a struggle for everyone, with fuel, food, and vehicles in short supply. The big bike manufacturers had also suffered during the war, and were not in a position to sponsor teams in the 1919 race. The first stage was 388 kilometers from Paris to Le Havre, and was won by Jean Rossius. However, the Belgian was handed a thirty-minute penalty for illegally helping Philippe Thys, which in turn moved Henri Pélissier into first. Pélissier held on to the lead for the next two stages, but then antagonized the other cyclists by comparing himself to a thoroughbred, and everybody else to workhorses.

The rest of the riders took their revenge on the fourth stage from Brest to Les Sables-d'Olonne when they attacked Pélissier and his brother Francis, who had stopped with a mechanical difficulty. The Pélissiers tried working with other riders to regain the leaders, until Desgrange put a stop to it. Pélissier ended up losing thirty-five minutes that day. Eugène Christophe took over the race lead, while the Pélissier brothers were so irate that they abandoned the race. Christophe hung on in through the Pyrénées and the Alps, and was still leading the race by the eleventh stage to Geneva.

After that stage, Christophe was awarded the first-ever yellow jersey by Desgrange; it made the race leader easily recognizable. The color was supposed to have been chosen to represent the color of the pages of *L'Auto,* but it was also said that yellow was used because no other dyes were available due to postwar shortages. It has since become one of the most iconic garments in sport. However, when Christophe appeared at the next stage wearing the jersey, he had to put up with name-calling from the other riders, who started referring to him as a canary.

Christophe would wear the jersey for the next three stages, but unfortunately suffered a misfortune very similar to the one that befell him in 1913. In that edition of the race his forks had broken on the Col du Tourmalet when he was in second place overall, and he famously had to run down the mountain to a village forge to repair them. He had lost hours that time. In 1919, with just two stages remaining, his lead of twenty-eight minutes over second-place Firmin Lambot seemed insurmountable. Then on the penultimate stage, to Dunkirk, his forks broke on a particularly tough section of cobbles, having been weakened from a crash earlier in the race. Six years after his last broken-fork incident, it took him just half the time to repair his bicycle, but it was enough to pass the lead to Lambot.

Lambot held on to win the race two days later in Paris, while Christophe finished in third overall. He ended up receiving the same prize money as Lambot, as *L'Auto* felt bad for him due to his misfortune. In addition, various donations were made by fans who also felt sorry for him; in the end, he made 13,310 francs, compared with 5,500 for Lambot. Christophe would never win the Tour, but he was forever remembered as the first yellow jersey wearer.

Of the sixty-seven riders who started, only eleven made it back to

Paris. Later, Paul Duboc was disqualified for getting a lift when an axle broke, leaving it as just ten finishers. It is the lowest number of finishers ever; in addition, the average speed was the slowest ever at just over twenty-four kilometers per hour. All of this was a reflection of the damage to the country's roads and to cyclists' fitness level.

The 1919 Tour de France was a struggle for both organizers and competitors. But what mattered was that the race had taken place. The Tour had survived and would continue uninterrupted until 1940, when it would be stopped by war again.

The effect that the First World War had on professional cycling was immense. On the one hundredth anniversary of the start of the war, in 2014, commemorations would take place in Germany, France, Britain, Belgium, and many other countries involved. As with the Circuit des Champs de Bataille back in 1919, the 2014 Tour de France would commemorate the war, with a stage start in Ypres, a stage finish in Reims, and routing through Verdun, Douaumont, Chemin des Dames, and Arras, where hundreds of thousands had lost their lives. The war had cost the lives of an estimated thirty-two Tour de France cyclists, in addition to countless other professional road and track cyclists. But their sacrifice has not been forgotten.

BIBLIOGRAPHY

Books

Bastide, Roger, *Petit-Breton: La belle epoque du cyclisme* (Denoel, 1985)

Beatty, Jack, *The Lost History of 1914 – Reconsidering the Year the Great War Began* (Walker and Company, 2012)

Behaeghe, Tillo, *Aimé Behaeghe – First Pilot in Central Africa* (Hanger Flying)

Bobet, Jean, *Lapize : Celui-là était un "as"* (La Table Ronde, 2003)

Bourgier, Jean-Paul, *Le Tour de France 1914: De la Fleur au Guidon à la Baïonnette* (Le Pas d'Oiseau, 2010)

Brown, Malcolm, *Verdun 1916* (Tempus Publishing, 1999)

Chany, Pierre, *La fabuleuse histoire du Tour de France* (Minerva, 2004)

Clayton, Anthony, *Paths of Glory – The French Army 1914 – 18* (Cassell, 2003)

Evans, Martin Marix, *Over the Top – Great Battles of the First World War* (Chartwell Books Inc., 2002)

Ferguson, Niall, *The Pity of War 1914 – 1918* (Penguin Books, 1998)

Foot, John, *Pedalare! Pedalare! – A History of Italian Cycling* (Bloomsbury Publishing, 2011)

Gilbert, Adrian, D., *Voices of the Foreign Legion* (Mainstream Publishing, 2009)

Gilbert, Martin, *The First World War – A Complete History* (Henry Holt and Company, 1994)

Guinness, Rupert, *Aussie Aussie Aussie, Oui, Oui, Oui – Australian Cyclists in 100 Years of the Tour de France* (Random House Australia, 2003)

Hart, Peter, *The Somme,* (Cassell, 2005)

Hastings, Max, *Catastrophe – Europe Goes to War 1914* (William Collins, 2013)

Hemingway, Ernest, *A Farewell to Arms* (Scribner, 1929)

Hochschild, Adam, *To End All Wars – A Story of Loyalty and Rebellion, 1914-1918* (Mariner Books, 2011)

Homan, Andrew, M., *Life in the Slipstream – The Legend of Bobby Walthour Sr.* (Potomac Books, 2011)

Leroy, Pascal, *François Faber : Du Tour de France au champ d'honneur,* (L'Harmattan, 2006)

McGann, Bill and Carol. *The Story of the Tour de France, Volume 1:1903-1964* (Dog Ear Publishing, 2006)

Ousby, Ian, *The Road to Verdun* (Jonathan Cape, 2002)

Price-Smith, Andrew T., *Contagion and chaos: disease, ecology, and national security in the era of globalization* (MIT Press, 2009)

Rockwell, Paul Ayres, *War Letters of Kiffin Yates Rockwell* (The Country Life Press, 1925)

Thompson, Christopher, S., *The Tour de France* (University of California Press, 2006)

Witherell, James, L., *When Heroes were Giants – 100 Tours de France* (Sunbury Press, 2013)

Newspapers

Examiner

La Gazzetta dello Sport

La Libre

L'Auto

The Farmer and Settler

The Guardian

The Independent

The New York Times

Websites

www.awm.gov.au

www.bikeraceinfo.com

www.cwgc.org

www.cyclingarchives.com

www.cyclingart.blogspot.ie

www.defense.gouv.fr/sante

www.history.com

www.memoire-du-cyclisme.eu

www.memorial-genweb.org

www.servicehistorique.sga.defense.gouv.fr

www.sportgeschiedenis.nl

www.sporza.be

www.svloches.e-monsite.com

www.telegraph.co.uk

Other cycling books from Breakaway:

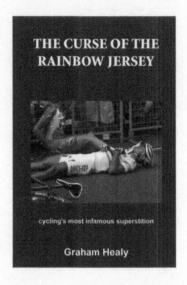

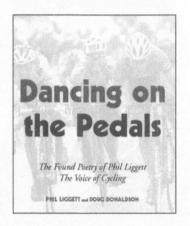

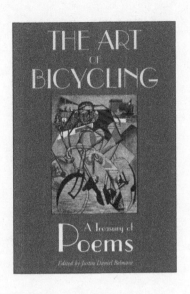

Available in bookstores and online.